Runes Rebooted
Runes for the Tech Age

Wendy Trevennor

GREEN MAGIC

Green Magic
53 Brooks Road
Street
Somerset
BA16 0PP
England

www.greenmagicpublishing.com

Designed & typeset by K.DESIGN
Winscombe, Somerset

ISBN 9781838132460

GREEN MAGIC

This book is lovingly dedicated to my wonderful Coven and outer circle, for their inspiration, their support and encouragement in all aspects of my life.

My thanks to my sister-in-law Lola Pash and my good friend Karen Thomas for their care and patience in proofreading and checking my work.

Contents

Introduction

My interest in runes has been relatively recent, but I now spend a lot of time kicking myself for not investing in them earlier. So simple and yet so complex, so easy to connect with and so useful for magic that you wonder why anyone bothers with anything else.

You might think, what possible relevance can the runes, a system in use in the Dark Ages, have for the modern pagan as he sits trawling his smartphone for information online to help him with day-to-day situations? Surely the use of those funny little stick shapes died out with the Vikings?

But I can tell you that the runes reach out from the past to the present and future like Bifrost, the mythical bridge to Asgard, and are just as relevant today as they were fifteen centuries ago to those on a spiritual path.

Leif Forkbeard might have worried a bit more about his crops and the defence of his homestead from marauders, and a bit less about his broadband connection, but he was a man with basically the same emotional makeup and day-to-day human concerns as Jayden Smith in IT who, like Leif, is currently working at home, in this case because of COVID-19, the pandemic that brought the world to a standstill in 2020–2021.

In this book we will examine what the runes were originally for and how they can guide or inform people's everyday lives then and now. We will see that while Leif may have worried about raiders carrying off his wife and setting fire to his house, and looked to the runes for guidance, Jayden's concerns about the spate of burglaries on his estate and the high incidence of computer viruses he has been attracting can also be addressed.

Since the basic needs of humans and their general desires and ambitions do not change fundamentally from era to era, we casually discard the wisdoms of the past at our peril. If we understand and heed them, the runes can advise and guide us in our activities and lives, just as they have always done for those wise enough to listen. *Runes Rebooted* is intended to highlight the relevance of runes to you and your concerns today, whether that be, 'Why does my PC keep crashing?' or, 'How can I find my ideal job?' or 'Where is my next meal coming from?'

Take a journey with me. We will take Raido and Ehwaz with us for transport, and Algiz for protection and Fehu for luck, and all the others as well, for their various properties. We will travel back into the past (where I'm afraid your smartphone won't work) and meet Leif and his family, before we return to the present with the information we have gained and put it to use on 21st century concerns.

Meet the Norse Gods who gave their influence to the runes, learn their legends and how they impact on the symbols – these timeless stories are still well loved today. Indeed, Thor himself has been the star of several CGI-enhanced movies in the last few years, thanks to Marvel Comics (actually, the comics were how I first met Thor and Loki when I was a child).

Then, hop in the time machine and we'll get back home to the 21st century and learn a bit more from people in our own time.

We will take a look at the meaning of each rune and try to really get to know each one. Please excuse any witchsplaining: this book is aimed not only at people with knowledge who want to brush up on runes, but also at people with less magical knowledge who are perhaps new to this whole area. Our remit is to capture this amazing system and apply it, lock, stock and ancient barrel, to our own time and needs, to the era of traffic jams, smartphones, social media and Covid.

One final note. The Norse runes have sadly been associated at some points in their history with racism, particularly in the 20th century. It is important to remember that most ancient societies knew little of this sorry attitude; they may have hated their enemies but cared little about the colour of their skins. As with individual personality defects, these mindsets arise from unhappy circumstances affecting nations as a sickness.

Those who are drawn to the runes in the present time need not be exclusively blonde-haired and blue-eyed Aryans. The runes are for all; black, white or any colour of skin in between. They have made it into the 21st century, where people of colour, women and people with alternate sexualities are all hopefully treated with respect and equality and are certainly protected by laws against stupid bigotry. No one raises an eyebrow at Kemetics, Western people who worship Egyptian Gods, so why should anyone object if a Japanese person, for example, takes an interest in the Norse runes? We're all Jock Thampson's bairns.

CHAPTER ONE

Let's Boot Up

So, who were these dudes that produced the runes and used them for magic and divination? They were a Germanic race who were around in the first millennium CE, worshipping their own pagan Gods and living in what is now Scandinavia. We all have a slightly comical image of the Norsemen (the Vikings were just the military wing) in our minds, somewhere between Hägar the Horrible and something from Assassin's Creed. Women don't seem to figure very prominently in this culture, which often appears to be largely about marauding, testosterone and drinking mead from oversized cow horns.

What we know about the Norsemen is limited to archaeological finds, accounts from historians of other cultures and the small amount of literature they left behind, very little of which was recorded contemporaneously. They did leave a lot of art as well, in six different recognised styles, but the images don't always come with metadata, so can be intriguing rather than enlightening. The Norsemen loved their tales, songs and poetry, but these were not written down until after their age had ended, though inscriptions on gravestones and other artefacts do survive. Compared to other civilisations – for example, Rome or Ancient Egypt – they left us almost nothing, and their literature was later bowdlerised by the Christian clerics who translated the tales and poems. The source for almost all our knowledge of Norse beliefs is two bodies of literature known as the Elder and Younger Eddas, also known as the Prose and Poetry Eddas. The Younger was written, or part-written, by Snorri Sturluson in the 13th century, and the Elder was certainly around at that time, but may be much older.

The Norsemen are still with us today; many people who identify as British (or Scottish, Irish, French, Spanish, Portuguese, Italian, Slavic or West Mediterranean) carry Viking DNA, either because their many-times-great grandmother had an adventure with a marauder or because they are descended from the Norsemen who stayed and settled, especially in the north-east of Britain.

And you will find that they are full of surprises, one of these being just how much they have influenced our modern culture. Folk customs that we vaguely think of as being Medieval or later have come to us from the Norsemen, from their considerable influence on our English language to many of our holiday customs, especially the imagery associated with Christmas and Santa Claus.

But of course, one of their major legacies is the runes. There is a timeless quality to them, the very simplicity of the symbols and the concepts they represent conjure up a glimpse of eternity such as you might experience on a quiet beach, playing with pebbles. It is a quality that has drawn magicians, witches and other magical practitioners and diviners over the centuries. The runes fascinate and, although they do not give up their secrets wantonly, they have the attraction of being simpler to learn than many systems.

To start with, a little bit of background on the runes: they span centuries of Western history. The first signs drawn by men were magical or spiritual symbols which had as yet no significance in the writing down of language, but served as amulets for the believers, markers for sacred places and quasi-heraldic devices for warlords. These symbol or glyph runes can still be found mixed in with alphabetic runes on carvings and bracteates – the beautiful golden 'medals' the Norsemen made in great quantities and wore as ornaments or tokens of rank. Very quickly the Norsemen realised the potential of these symbols for passing on messages, marking boundary posts and even writing letters. The oldest runic alphabet may go back to the time of Christ, but the amazing thing is that they are still alive and kicking today. The 20th century saw a great revival of interest in them, fuelled by the growth of neopaganism and not least by the author JRR Tolkien, who used them extensively in his fantasy fiction works *The Hobbit* and *The Lord of the Rings*. Many of us were introduced to the symbols in the hand-drawn illustrations of this revered author, who has had such an influence on the generations following the publication of his works.

Sadly, the other group that showed an interest in them was the German Nazi Party, many of whom had an interest not only in what they perceived as their 'pure' race's culture (ridiculous, as we now know we nearly all have DNA from many races in our makeup) but in the occult, and the use of the runes for magic. This may have discouraged later use of the runes by others, who perhaps saw them as tainted with the odious philosophies of Hitler and his like, but Tolkien did a lot to erase that, associating them in many people's minds with his major work – which many have seen as an allegory of World War II.

The old runemasters believed that the runes came courtesy of Odin, who dredged them from the Well of Wyrd after undergoing a painful ordeal lasting nine days; hanging upside down from the cosmic tree Yggdrasil (this is thought to be the origin of the Hanged Man card in The Tarot), pierced by his own spear. In the ancient *Lay of Havamal* he speaks of what he has learned from the runes and the powers they have given him, and even claims, 'A twelfth (enchantment) I know: if I see in a tree a corpse hanging from a rope, I can so write and colour the runes, that it will come down and talk to me.'

What always strikes me is that Odin himself must care about his runes, as they have survived centuries of Christianity, with clerics always being deeply suspicious of their pagan origins and meanings, and keen to make them victims of cancel culture, to arrive in the 21st century intact and still meaningful.

The runes date back to at least as early as 150CE, when the earliest runic inscriptions were made, and they may date back as early as the first century BCE; there is currently no way of knowing. The Roman historian Tacitus mentions seeing what seems to be the runes being used for divination in an account of 98BCE, but he forgot to take any photographs. Their origins are obscure, though scholars have put forward the Italian alphabets called Rhaetic and Etruscan, Latin, Phoenician or Greek alphabets as their source – the earliest form of the rune Sowelu (S) certainly resembles a slightly stretched Sigma. The Norsemen got around, piling up their equivalent of frequent flyer miles – but it is also true that a person sitting down to design a writing system is going to come up with many of the same shapes as the chap down the valley doing the same thing, because letters need to be kept simple and there are only so many shapes you can make on a bit of wood with a stick of charcoal.

The first incarnation was the alphabet known as Futhark (from the first six letters), which was used by the Germanic peoples in Europe and what we now call Scandinavia, and this is the one that witches and mystics tend to use because it is the oldest and therefore the purest. It is not like Microsoft Windows where you get improvements at each update; with runes, you stick with the original because they don't get better and smarter, just different. To my mind, using the later runic alphabets (runes v2.0) is like getting your news from social media clickbait sites instead of from organisations that do actual news gathering (Reuters, BBC, etc). The newer sources may be worked over and glitzy, but maybe not as relevant, accurate or fresh from the source – and of course, peppered with ads!

By the 8th century, changes had been made to the original system; the newer Scandinavian runic alphabet called the Younger

Futhark had evolved, to be followed by the Anglo-Saxon variant Futhorc, and several others as well. It is as well to know your way around some of these later runes, 'just in case', but for the purposes of this book we will go with the older system.

Then, like a vanguard of early Jehovah's Witnesses, the Christians came a-knocking, brought in the first instance on the coattails of the Roman Empire, which was always a tolerant conduit for non-Roman faiths and also brought Mithras and Isis to Britain. In the sixth century, further waves of Christians arrived, led by St Columba and Augustine, later the Archbishop of Canterbury. Where the Romans showed tolerance for other faiths, the Christians most emphatically did not. They set about expunging all the native belief systems, although they tolerated the runes for a while (eventually they banned them, not just because of their pagan origins but because they were used for magic and divination as well as everyday writing).

Pagan sacred places were ruthlessly annexed and built on, crosses were carved into sacred stones and pagan festivals were appropriated and whitewashed – midwinter was Freyr's birthday, not Christ's, but getting the local heathens along to a rebranded jolly was always going to be easier than just banning their own holidays.

The Norse Gods sank from sight, their only remaining traces the names of our days of the week, but the runes carried on, being used in Christian scripts through the Mediaeval period, and indeed some of the later forms of runes continued in use in Scandinavia into the 20th century, and also in Austria, where a new runic system was designed.

The revival of interest that happened in the 20th century saw the publication of the very first book on the runes as a spiritual tool, published by anthropologist Ralph Blum in 1982 and including a set of ceramic runes in a plush bag. For many of us, this was the first experience we had with them.

As neopaganism bloomed through the 20th century and into the 21st, pagan streams based exclusively on Norse beliefs arose, and the runes were launched again into mainstream interest.

Nowadays they are not used for writing letters, signposts or shopping lists, at least, not by any well-known groups, but they are again very much used for some of their original purposes: for magic and divination. Strikingly magical looking and easy to draw, they are ideal for creating amulets and charms, and are a great deal easier to learn than the Tarot, with its 78 oracle cards in two groups. And because the shapes are simple, they suit magical secrecy: a rune inscribed on your phone with nail polish or worn around your neck for luck will not usually be recognised as magical by a muggle and, if questioned, can easily be explained away as a good luck charm or a fanciful embellishment of an initial.

So, let's schedule a meet-up with the Elder Futhark runes over coffee over the next few chapters. Lurking in the background of the symbols will be a set of movers and shakers we will meet in the third chapter: the Gods themselves, figures in the runic landscape that have a strong bearing on their meanings and use.

They have a couple of mutual friends too: Jayden Smith and Leif Forkbeard, two men divided by time but pretty much the same kind of dude at heart, and both are pagans: let's hop in the Rardis (runic time machine) and go meet them now.

691 East Jutland

Hail, I am Leif; welcome to my farmstead. Like my father before me and his father before him, I own this land and the ashes of my forefathers lie in the soil here. I grow grain and keep cows, pigs, goats and fowls.

When I was born, the Norn[1] decreed that I would be strong, should dedicate myself to Freyr, and also that I should read the runes. These are an ancient and deeply sacred oracle for my people, and there are runemasters

---

1   Norn: see Chapter Three: Figures in a Runic Landscape.

who travel from village to village with the runes, bringing their wisdom. There was a runemaster in the village when I was young, and he taught me all about the staves, what they mean and how they speak to you, and he showed me how to make my own set, with my own blood and with wood cut from the living branch. When I was a child, I wished to be one of them, a runemaster myself, but it was not to be: my father grew old and his joints pained him, and I was a dutiful son, so I stayed home and helped him with the land and the animals.

I have my own set and never a dawn passes but I draw a stave from the pouch and see what the day is bringing. I use the runes to help me make decisions: plant barley or rye? Ask the runes. I asked the runes who to marry, and am very fortunate in my wife Frida, who works hard on the farm and has given me four strong children.

I live two days' ride from Aarhus, in a shallow valley that keeps us sheltered from the winds that blow across the land. My house is simple, but it fills my needs. It is made from timber and withies and plastered with earth, and the roof is thatched with sedge. My great grandfather built it, but it has needed maintenance work over the years, another task I have to do. I have one hired man to help me; he sleeps by the fire at night. My father never had anyone to help except my mother, and later my brothers and me, but my sons are too young to do more than play at farming.

Frida tends the family shrine, but I make sure the image of Freyr is specially cared for, with beer and food before Him every day. He has been good to me in so many ways. I honour Odin and the other Gods as well, but Freyr is the God to whom I cleave. I have His runes Fehu and Ingwaz over the lintel and use other runes as well in my day-to-day life, runes for protection and happiness, runes for good crops and prosperity, runes to keep my family well. I was so fortunate to have that early teaching from a master when I was young, which has stayed with me and blessed my life. These little bits of wood have such power in them that I, a common ceorl, can make my life so good that I envy no one, not my neighbour, not the Earl.

2021 London

Hi, my name's Jayden and I work in IT, for a biggish company based in London and Bangalore. I'm a software dev, and I live in a tiny flat in north London with my girlfriend Amber; we've been together two years now and she's pretty cool — pretty hot too! I have been a pagan since my teens, when I started reading about it and watching YouTube videos on Heathenry. Living in London, I don't get much chance to get out there with the re-enactment guys, but my beliefs mean a lot to me, and the runes are one way I can keep in touch with them. Ma had the Ralph Blum set in the 1990s, when she was young, and I found them when I was a kid and that seemed to spark my interest. I made my own set a few years ago, and sat in on a couple of webinars (Runes 101 if you like) on how to use them, but I don't flash them around at work... Paganism doesn't go down too well in a professional environment, so I stay in the broom closet. Doesn't stop me practising, at work as well as at home, but I find muggles[2] are easily fobbed off with some excuse if they catch you out doing something that they consider a bit weird.

Before Covid I always attended the local moot — that's, like, a get-together in the pub for pagans, usually with a talk on something. It's cool; used to be all woolly old guys with crumbs in their beards and real ale, whatever that is, LOL, but as time goes on, I've seen more Millennials like me coming along. But the moot went into hibernation with Covid, though we stayed in touch through Facebook — the organiser is one of the woolly ones, and I guess at that age it's Facebook or nada.

My special deity is Odin; He's the head honcho when it comes to knowledge and even IT. He's really dope. I honour Him by wearing the Valknutt (Odin's symbol) under my shirt, and I had thought about getting a tat based on it (but Amber whined about the idea, saying it looked gross) until I gave it up. She can talk... all those swirly things and butterflies and crap. I have an altar set up to Him at home in a corner of the bedroom,

---

2   I am indebted to the author J K Rowling for her invention of this word, now universally used by pagans to refer to non-magical or non-pagan people.

but it's nothing I can't sweep into a drawer if Amber's muggle friends or her parents visit.

I have the Valknutt and a few runes on the base of my laptop too; 'cos no one ever sees the bottom of your lappy, right? The case is dark brown, and I painted them on really small in dark grey, so they don't exactly show up anyway. The same with my phone, though I was careful to make them as small as possible, as your phone gets left lying around on desks and stuff. I guess I could put runes on them both and cover them with a sticker, but that looks a bit girly. The runes I have on my devices are protective ones like Algiz and knowledge ones like Kenaz; they seem to work pretty well.

I've said my beliefs mean a lot to me, but I haven't told many of my friends about it because they would all think it was like Harry Potter or something. And I guess, in some way, it is. What's so awesome is what it can do for you: the runes are, like, the best magical tool, with centuries of power and meaning and stuff. Just awesome.

And now, let's get on and meet the stars, the runes themselves.

CHAPTER TWO

The Gods' Own Alphabet

The 24 runes of the Elder Futhark are divided into three families (or Aetts) of eight runes each, and each Aett has a patron deity. This is what they look like:

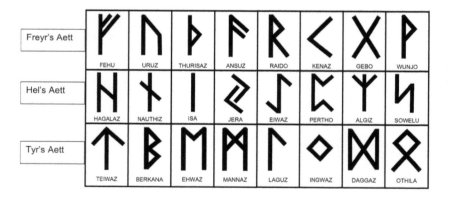

As I have mentioned, the runes mutated over time into several alphabets, which were in use across Scandinavia and Western Europe, including Britain. The systems all have their own rune poems, which can all be found towards the back of this book in Appendix One, but a great deal of study (and imagination) is needed to wrest much meaning out of these mysterious haiku-like verses. There are three: the Anglo-Saxon, which is the oldest, the Norwegian and the Icelandic, all of which are reproduced. Unfortunately, there is no rune poem specifically for the Elder Futhark, but that of the Anglo-Saxon Futhorc covers the same phonetic sounds, even if the letters have slightly different names. The rune alphabets vary considerably as the letters have changed so much over the years, some being added, some being changed or dropped altogether as the languages and their pronunciations spread and changed. Sticking to the Elder Futhark means that you only need to bother with the Anglo-Saxon rune poem, which is a little easier to understand, though the other two have contributions to make as well. These verses often seem very obscure and even irrelevant; the use of kennings[3] and the lost knowledge surrounding the runes makes these very difficult to understand, but there is meaning if you study them assiduously. As with all such oracles, more can be wrung from them if you spend time with them and meditate on them. Often, they may even jump out at you with their meaning. Have patience – it isn't always meant to be easy.

It can sometimes seem that the runes overlap with their meanings: Uruz, Thurisaz and Hagalaz, for example, all speak of sudden disasters, but each rune has layer upon layer of meanings, and as you explore each one, it opens up and shows you more and more. A good way to get to know them all is to carry one with you, in your pocket or your handbag, and also in your mind, until it speaks to you and gives up its meanings – I was going to say, 'all its meanings', but I'm not sure that ever happens.

The order of the runes is not always generally agreed, apart from the first six. The last two runes, Othila and Daggaz, seem to be particularly interchangeable. The very oldest carving of the whole runic order is on a 4th century gravestone found in Gotland, Sweden. This gives Othila as the last rune, and some rune

---

3   See Chapter Three for an explanation of kennings.

scholars place it last, as I have done, because of its meaning of homecoming. Others set Daggaz as the last rune because it is to do with a completed cycle, and perhaps because it then sits opposite Jera on the runic Wheel of the Year, and Daggaz seems to fit better with either of the solstices than does Othila.

In each case I will give you the pronunciation of the rune's name and an image that will help you learn and remember its shape and meaning. I will also suggest ways in which the runes can indicate a person in your life. There are times when we need answers that concern a specific individual; perhaps asking to whom we might best turn for advice or help, or which person is being indicated by a message from other runes.

AETT ONE

The first one is Freyr's Aett, and kicks off with his own rune Fehu. But you cannot expect all the runes in an Aett to follow the God that rules them, so as well as this positive and comforting rune, this Aett also includes scary beasts like Uruz and Thurisaz. There are supposed to be relationships between all the runes in an Aett and in the order in which they stand, but it is easier to think of them *all* being related, and to just notice special relationships as and when they occur. The first Aett includes a lot of *incidents*: challenge, misfortune, celebration, message.

Fehu (F) riches

PRONOUNCE FAY-hoo

ASSOCIATIONS Freyr and Freyja, Njörd the Sea God,
Nerthus the Earth Goddess, Frigga, Audhumla the
Cosmic Cow Who Created Life

 This one used to bother me a bit. It looks too much like another F-shaped rune called Ansuz: so much so that I have even seen an experienced rune reader get them mixed up while doing a demonstration at a pagan moot. One easy way to sort them out in your mind is to have a mental picture of Fehu as a cow's horns. For Fehu is about cows... about richness and riches; you can think of it as the *butter rune*. To the Norsemen, a lot of cows were the equivalent of a big fat bank balance and a job with a telephone number salary. Leif considers himself pretty well-off because he has four cows on his East Jutland farm; he is a ceorl (churl, or freeman). Jayden's equivalent position is owning his own tiny London flat with a small mortgage and a lot of equity, and having a generous salary with his job in IT.

The Norsemen didn't know about cholesterol and to them Fehu spoke of beef, butter, milk and cheese, and plenty of them... in clover, we might say today. We also use the expression 'cash cow'. It was how they measured their worldly goods and their fortune. Turn up Fehu and you might well expect a pay rise, or some other piece of good fortune. The Norsemen carried this rune for good luck, and so can you.

This rune personifies Freyr, the Norse God of Abundance we met in Chapter One, blonde and handsome and carrying a sheaf of corn and an antler (he gave away his sword for love). Yummy. Freyr represents the sun-soaked earth, fields of waving corn, greenery, livestock, abundance.

Although it is one of the most positive runes, Fehu carries two important warnings: one is that wealth for its own sake is a trap that will lead to unhappiness, that wealth should be shared with the tribe or used to do good. And there is the warning that such wealth and prosperity breeds not only arrogance and selfishness in the holder, but envy and anger in others. The Norsemen appear to have thought very much in terms of the community and the common good, and this colours a lot of the runes, where today we might think more in terms of our own good alone.

If your answer is about a person, this is going to indicate someone who has deep pockets who is, as we say, *not short of a bob or two,* and is also benevolent, able and willing to help someone who is really deserving. The rune refers to movable wealth, by the way, not property, which comes under Othila. This is about what you have got in the bank or in the cupboard, or round your neck or on your wrists, fingers or earlobes, or in your wallet.

Most of the runes are reversible, and when reversed they can carry different meanings: this is called a **murkstave** (often spelled merkstave) and some runemasters acknowledge it and some do not. Later on, we will discuss how to make up your mind on that one. The Fehu murkstave may be about the consequences of arrogant and selfish prosperity, or about poverty. It can speak of a greed for wealth for its own sake (the Norsemen referred to gold as *strife metal*).

Leif and Jayden both believe in the runes, and every morning they draw one from the bag to see what the day will bring.

Leif: My cows must all be pregnant!
Jayden: My contract is being renewed!

Uruz (U) challenge, ordeal

PRONOUNCE OO-ruz

ASSOCIATIONS Njörd and Thor

Yeah, another cow rune, but what a different one.

Until the 17th century the forests of northern Europe were stalked by a terrifying creature called the aurochs; it would make your average angry farm bull look like a Pekinese. Julius Caesar described it as not much smaller than an elephant – and don't forget: the Romans knew elephants. It was a wild bovine that stood around two metres tall at the shoulder with metre-long horns – and just in case it needed to be any scarier, it had the personality of an attack dog.

The Norsemen saw it as the ideal opportunity to prove their manhood: their young men went out hunting it and returned (if they were lucky) with its horns as trophies, not to mention a severe case of PTSD.

Challenge, ordeal and initiation are all included in the meanings of this rune. You have deliberately gone to find this monster in the forest, and there it is, in your path; a terrifying creature that sets your knees knocking so hard they get bruises, yet you must overcome and pass it if you ever hope to be taken seriously again by your tribe. This is put up or shut up time, and you will be tested to the max. Just what form this testing may take will be suggested by nearby runes, yet Uruz and what it brings is vital for your personal growth and progress. Your tribe will be there supporting you and, whatever you endure, others have endured it before you and come through triumphantly. And as Nietzsche said: '*Whatever does not kill me makes me stronger*'.

This could refer to a challenging rite of passage, or some other ominous situation, including a court case, a crisis in your personal life, a taxing job interview, a gruelling exam or even an ethical dilemma (we say 'on the horns of a dilemma'). In the bad old days before update patches, I might have suggested a system upgrade. The physical aspect of fighting the aurochs speaks of physical training or hardening, preparation perhaps for a sporting event. For a woman, it could mean childbirth: a painful and exhausting ordeal that culminates in joy.

If a single person is indicated, it is someone who will put you through an ordeal, though it may be for your own good: a strict teacher, a stern boss, perhaps a very overbearing parent who expects what you feel is too much from you. This may well be a person of whom you are honestly afraid, even though you may have great respect for them.

With all the runes, there are layers upon layers upon layers of meaning. When they had been killed, the horns of the aurochs were cleaned, polished and lined with silver for use as drinking horns, which brings the idea of trophies earned at some cost into this rune.

The origin for the shape of this rune is hard to identify, but I see it as the outline of a hulking great animal like a woolly mammoth or a huge hairy bull, perhaps dimly glimpsed through the mist, a danger and a challenge you must get past. The animal stands for pure power, and magically this rune can be useful in adding a good bash to your spellwork, bringing the power of the animal and its symbol into what you are doing.

Murkstave: Difficulty in facing the challenge, failure, suffering, particularly fear.

Leif: Thor protect me; the Earl wants me to go viking with him seeking
  plunder! It's a big honour... but oo-er!
Jayden: Uh-oh, the boss wants me to take on the Readibank database
  corruption issues — no one has been able to sort that out! But if I
  succeed, it would mean a promotion for sure.

Thurisaz (TH) sudden bad news

PRONOUNCE THOOR-is-saz
ASSOCIATIONS Thor and his hammer Mjöllnir, Loki

At first glance, this rune looks quite similar to the threat of Uruz. Thurisaz means 'giant' or 'thorn' in the old Germanic languages, and either way it is a painful thing to encounter. But there is no challenge this time and nothing to be gained, just a warning that something nasty is on its way to you. See this shape as a nasty thorn right in the middle of a twig. Ouch!

The shape of this rune may be based on Thor's war-hammer Mjöllnir, a symbol that is now commonly worn as jewellery or tattoos by members of the pagan streams that honour the Norse Gods. And this carries on the giant theme, for Thor's favourite target was the skull of any giant that got in his way! So, this rune has a dual meaning: it can be something dangerous, but that very thing could also be a protection – Mjöllnir has a handle as well as a head.

The Norse Gods had a strange relationship with the giants; sometimes they loved them and had children with them – Freyr famously gave up his magical sword to win the heart of a beautiful giantess called Gerda – and the line generally between God and giant was quite blurred. But most of the time, the Gods hated and distrusted them and fought wars to contain them. Giants were seen as hostile, mischievous and generally negative beings, the forces of Chaos embodied. Remember that the God Loki was not technically a member of the Aesir but a giant (as the Norsemen recognised ancestry through the father's line) and he was a fairly nasty piece of work who, amongst other misdemeanours, caused the death of the innocent and beloved God Baldr, apparently just out of spite.

If Thurisaz is translated as 'thorn', the situation remains the same. We speak of 'a thorn in our side' when talking about a painful problem. Could another meaning for this be a thorn in the sense of a hurtful remark made to us by an unkind person? Some people are quite sensitive to this kind of thing and may feel the 'wound' for days afterwards. Looking at the other side of the rune (the handle end), could it be you who has caused the hurt to someone else?

In terms of people, the rune speaks of someone you will not exactly welcome with open arms. This is the bully, the pain in the butt, the nasty in-law, the bane of your life, someone who has caused you grief in the past and looks likely to go on doing so, someone who seems to take pleasure in making your life miserable.

So, what we are looking at here is analogous to the attack of an enemy. Of course, in 21st century Britain we don't have to worry about Erik Bloodaxe from the next valley roaring down on us with all his hairy and heavily armed hordes, but we have enough unpleasant challenges of our own to fill this role: neighbours from hell, bullying at work, a road accident, a worrying medical diagnosis, even an assault by a mugger or a drunk. The problem may even involve a large faceless organisation such as County Hall making an attack on your lifestyle in some way, unassailable as they always are.

Thurisaz may refer to any area of your life. In romance it could mean your relationship is under threat; perhaps your partner is about to leave, or it could just be a massive row brewing. I personally see this rune as referring to a one-off bad event, perhaps involving violence and certainly physical or emotional pain. It could be a nasty illness. It could be as trivial as a toothache – though it must be said that there is little to compare with a bad toothache for making your life utter misery. But it can also mean the eruption of a long-standing inconvenience or pain.

The rune also carries the meaning that you must show endurance: it's no good throwing your toys out of the pram. You must hang in there, must show fortitude and patience to overcome the problem, and not dissolve into a little wet heap of frustration or fear before it if you wish to get through.

Two of the rune poems mention women; the Norwegian poem states, 'Giant causes the sickness of women'. I don't fully understand this meaning, unless it refers to rape, a common danger for women in the violent Dark Ages. Thurisaz also has layers of sexual meanings, including male sexuality and aggression, and while this is less of a threat to women today, it is still there. I cannot imagine the rune's function is to tell a woman she can expect menstrual cramps.

Murkstave: being overwhelmed by misfortune, the illness of women associated with fertility and reproduction.

Leif: My crops have been attacked by a disease!
Jayden: Oh crap, my laptop has a virus!

Ansuz (A) breath, communication, inspiration

PRONOUNCE AHN-sooz
ASSOCIATIONS Odin; murkstave Loki

 This rune refers to Odin's actions in giving life to the first man and woman by breathing into their mouths. As we have seen, its shape is easily confused with Fehu: to tell them apart, remember Fehu as a cow's horns (see picture with Fehu rune) and Ansuz as a pine tree – closely associated in our modern minds with breathing fresh air.

Sometimes called the Messenger Rune, it speaks of communication of all sorts, face-to-face speech, meetings, letters, phone calls and texts, emails, news stories, posts on Facebook and WhatsApp, tweets on Twitter and videos on YouTube and TikTok. It speaks of the power of words, to harm or heal, to deliver or destroy... we all know the pleasant feeling of seeing 'likes' on something we have posted, or the much less pleasant one of being on the receiving end of trolling. And in a non-virtual setting, words can do the same, encouraging or supporting a friend, or harming; whether that is by verbal violence, spreading nasty stories or just boring the pants off someone by talking too much.

If the question concerns a person, this rune indicates a messenger, someone coming with a communication in some shape or form, maybe ranging from urgently needed technical advice to common gossip. Or they may be a teacher, someone very wise and knowledgeable who will prove a mentor to you – life often sends people like this into our lives when we are younger, but they may still appear later in life. It could even mean that moment when you hear, perhaps on a bus or in the street, some words that set you right on your course, a revelation sent by the Gods.

Our English word 'inspiration' is based on the Latin word for breathing, and the rune also covers all kinds of art, music, poetry and literature: all arts that communicate feelings and meanings. One should also bear in mind the importance of the breath in spiritual practices, of the variety of breathing techniques used in meditation and preparation for prayer, from the Indian OM, which has been described as the Universe breathing, to pranic breath, the square breathing commonly practised by meditators and the Druidic Arwen. Such breathing exercises may benefit the soul as much as the body. Ansuz's appearance may be a message that you are ready to delve deeper into these mysteries to empower and enlighten yourself.

Murkstave: misinformation, lies, falsehood, confusion, beguiling words and deceit, betrayal of secrets.

Leif: A message from my cousin Arne; he's coming to visit.
Jayden: Expecting an email from my sister, catching me up on family news.

RAIDO (R) the journey, control

PRONOUNCE RYE-do
ASSOCIATIONS Thor and Odin

Just as it sounds, Raido, sometimes Raidho, comes from the verb to ride, now a leisure activity for the privileged, then a definition of travel. On one level it speaks of the journey of life, on a more mundane level of actual journeys and travel in the physical sense; perhaps a holiday or a necessary trip for business or family, or an adventure or just the making of progress.

The shape of this rune is easy to remember, as it's just like our own letter R — R for reins or riding. Reins mean control as well as travel. In fact, a better word for this rune in the 21st century might be 'driving', not just as in driving a car, but in driving work or politics or a relationship.

The Norsemen weren't exactly known for staying close to home; they loved to go off marauding and pillaging, returning home with riches, livestock and no doubt a comely wench or two, and they had a certain amount of disdain for anyone who stayed under the duvet instead of getting out there. Such lazy or cowardly people were only fit for a 'straw death' (the opposite of a glorious one in battle).

But we are also reminded of Odin, who never seems to spend any time at home, but is always off travelling the worlds with his battered old wideawake on his head, his ravens on his shoulders and his wolves at his heels. He knows that nothing is to be gained by inaction, and his rune speaks of the necessity for broadening the mind – not just by accumulating air miles but by way of books, study and the internet, to develop our minds and our own spirituality.

Broadening the mind, with all that implies, can be an important meaning of this rune, which is far from being all about physical travel. Broaden your mind to the rights and happiness of others, move away from narrow thinking, prejudice and preconceptions, move on from old ideas, think differently.

The runes are all interconnected, of course, but there are some more obvious relationships between some than others. There is a strong relationship between this rune and number 19, Ehwaz the horse rune, which we will be looking at later. While Ehwaz refers to the horse specifically, as a beast of burden or harness, Raido refers to the act of riding itself, or the act of travelling by any means. It can refer to travel in other realms, dreamwork and shamanism.

Then, as now, riding labelled you as someone who was someone, perhaps even an Earl or King, as horses weren't usually owned by the poor. The act of holding the reins also implies the act of leadership, of being in control, of mastery. The rune says, 'lead by example' and 'actions speak louder than words'. This may announce the arrival of a leader, one who will take charge of the situation and resolve matters with their authority. This is a person to whom you should look for an example.

Raido is the rune of protection while travelling and will warn of hidden dangers along the route. Magically, it is used as an amulet rune or as part of a bind rune to bring protection in travel.

Murkstave: being stuck in a rut, hampered, unable to make progress, a failed or wasted journey.

Leif: Time to travel to Aarhus to sell my weaned calves.

Jayden: Got a trip to our South Shields office coming up... quite a drive, and gotta take charge of an operation when I get there.

KENAZ (K) light, enlightenment, ability

PRONOUNCE KEN-az

ASSOCIATIONS Surtr, Heimdallr, Freyr and Freyja

The name of this rune is related to the ancient English word 'ken', as in 'beyond our ken', to the German word 'kennen' and the Scottish dialect word 'ken' which mean 'to know'. In many languages this is used to mean 'can', to which it may be related etymologically. In the Cornish language, for example, one says, *My a woer lywya, gwia, jynnskrifa*: 'I know how to drive, knit, type', meaning, I *can* do these things. This brings the meaning of ability into this rune, as well as knowledge. Bringing up this rune may indicate that you *can* do something.

In Anglo Saxon, Kenaz translates as 'torch' and is referred to as such in the A-S rune poem. The later rune poems render it as 'Kauna', which translates as ulcer. The shape of the rune could be the bulge of a swelling caused by infection, or it could be the beam of a torch – but you must bear in mind that a Norseman's torch was a burning branch taken from the fire or a stick dipped in pine pitch and wouldn't cast a shaped beam like a modern LED torch. However, this is a very useful image to take for this rune and speaks of the light and enlightenment that it signifies.

My gut feeling about this is to go with the older version, just as I would go with the Older Futhark alphabet rather than the later versions. But at the same time, I would bear this later meaning in mind in case the torch translation did not seem relevant — you learn to interpret the runes through all their levels of meaning and allusion. And of course, the burning implied by the older meaning could equally well imply the heat of fever or an injury caused by heat.

Kenaz is about fire and light, domesticated and put to use, and the benefits it brings. Its mundane meaning is fire and light in all their forms, from the cosy hearth to the brilliance of 21st century streetlights. The element of fire includes technology, including IT, so this is another rune with Ansuz that can speak of knowledge gained this way, for it is the rune of enlightenment. Again, think of its Dark Ages origins, when light was not simply a matter of flicking a switch or speaking to your home system, but had to be produced using a wooden drill, kindling and patience. In times when the darkness was unpolluted, it was real darkness, lit only by the Moon and stars on cloudless nights. This brings in an additional meaning, that enlightenment is not free; it must be worked for, just as the comfort of a fire has to be. Enlightenment and knowledge do not come without hard work and sacrifice, even if that sacrifice is just one of time.

This rune's meanings include all the qualities of fire: warmth, whether that means simple domestic comfort or the warmth of friendship and family; light, from a simple taper or phone torch to creative inspiration and the Road to Damascus experience of St Paul. It can also mean the fire of human passion: we say 'holding a torch' for someone; many of the runes have layers of erotic and sexual meaning. It can be a passionate commitment in some other way, for example to a political cause.

In Iron Age societies the blacksmith and his art were considered magical and sacred; oaths were sworn while touching an iron object, and to this day we feel that items like horseshoes are lucky in some way. Artistic inspiration and the work involved in crafts are another meaning of this rune, particularly arts that require heat in some way, such as glass blowing, pokerwork or throwing pots.

As we have seen before, the runes are firmly based in a community ethos, and usually include the meaning that what is for you, is for all. The torch that lights your path must also be held high, so that others can see to walk and share what you have found. If you have light and others do not, it is your God-given duty to light their way. Keeping light or knowledge to yourself really isn't cool. And as the suddenly lit landscape is transformed, so transformation is another meaning of Kenaz.

To come to the second meaning of Kenaz, when it becomes Kauna (ulcer) in later versions of the runes, this is an obvious warning about illness, infection or injury. But it could also speak a warning about the dangers of straying from what you understand into darker territory and ways not designed for your well-being. Personally, I think it could work to take this value of the rune for the **murkstave**, so that the reversed rune has this negative and ominous meaning. The given meaning for the murkstave is both the blockage of the light of knowledge, thus the darkness of ignorance, and the destructive power of fire, including the heat of fever, but you must never forget that the runes will show you many more meanings than you will find in a book or on a website. The murkstave of this rune looks like a sideways turn, so that the point of the stave faces right.

Kenaz is a lucky rune which can be carried for luck, and magically it also increases (fires up) the power of a rune sending. It is used to gain insights and uncover secrets, and to increase willpower and confidence. Its meaning of ability also informs this as a magical sigil.

Leif: I have prayed and received no answer; today the Gods spoke to me!
Jayden: I've just realised what is wrong with my Wi-Fi!

GEBO (hard G, as in 'gate') gift

PRONOUNCE GAY-bo
ASSOCIATIONS Odin and Frigga

This, with Wunjo, forms the end of the first Aett, and aren't they a lovely pair? Gebo means 'gift'... but it would be a big mistake to take this as the total meaning, put the rune back in the bag and go off smiling thinking that a big shiny parcel is on its way to you. This rune carries other meanings too, positive though they may be. And of course, it can also mean giving a gift, as well as receiving one.

See the rune as a kiss on a parcel, labelled by someone who has sent you a loving gift. But remember, it's a cross... so the gift should be reciprocated.

Gebo's mundane and basic meanings include a gift, blessing, opportunity, a love match (where rings and promises are given), a partnership, or a debt to be repaid. This last one doesn't sound quite so positive, and you must remember that the runes all have these nuances of reciprocity and sharing. If someone gave you a gift, they most certainly expected one in return – this was the custom in the Norsemen's time – and if you failed to match their generosity, you lost not only the friendship and co-operation of the person who gave you a gift, but perhaps more importantly for the Norsemen, you lost face. Generosity was seen then – as it is now – as one of the noblest of virtues, with selfishness and meanness being seen as despicable. So Gebo always speaks of reciprocity; that giving gifts will bring its own rewards, not just gifts in return, but friendship, goodwill and the satisfaction of having made someone else happy. And the gift doesn't have to be something solid, like chocolates or wine: it can be something abstract, like a promise or a favour — which will also hopefully be reciprocated in due course.

Charity is a word the Christians seem to have invented and certainly seen as of great importance in their way of life, yet the generosity of better-off people in all cultures to their friends and followers or to the poor has always been admired. Sharing was always the way in Norse society, so we can take the rune to also mean the giving of money or goods to charity, or to those less well-off than ourselves, perhaps the handing of a sandwich or soda to a homeless person or taking tins of food to a food bank, because you can and because both the giving and receiving of the gift blesses both giver and receiver. Many of us certainly take the regular giving to charity as a part of our spiritual duties, or if we do not, then perhaps this rune could be a suggestion that we should do so.

Odin himself encouraged this idea, often turning up on doorsteps in disguise to receive either a cordial welcome or a rebuff — both later rewarded as they deserved, a good illustration of the way this rune returns upon itself.

Gebo can also mean a gift to the Gods, a sacrifice or a sacred vow, or the paying of a debt or promise. One of the sources of our knowledge of the Norsemen's creative ability with metalwork, woodwork and other arts and crafts comes from the large amounts of offerings they left in sacred places, graves, bogs and lakes; of weapons and jewellery.

Love and partnerships are included in this sense of a bond implied in the exchange of items: rings in a marriage, perhaps a kiss, which is also sometimes used as the sealing of a bargain. The X sign could be seen as the crossed arms of men cutting their wrists and swearing blood-brotherhood by mixing their blood. Heavy stuff… and not a curly ribbon in sight.

Gifts can also mean those you were born with — in English we talk about someone's 'gifts', meaning their abilities and talents —

and even the gift of life itself. So, the rune speaks of the gifts given us by the Gods, as well as the gifts we should return to them, perhaps by passing the gifts on to others, showing empathy, compassion and forgiveness. And as one of my students pointed out, this can include voting in an election – we vote for a candidate and expect the gift of his promise of action in return. And if he reneges, we can take back our gift by voting for someone else next time.

Murkstave: there is no murkstave for Gebo; it is not reversible. However, it can be coloured by nearby runes in a cast, and possible adverse meanings include blockage in the area of giving and receiving in your life, or a misuse of your gifts.

Leif: I must find a fitting gift for my neighbour; he has given me the loan of his bull, which will ensure milk in the coming year.
Jayden: Grant sorted out my networking problem. I owe him big time.

WUNJO (V or W) joy, celebration

PRONOUNCE VOON-yo
ASSOCIATIONS Freyr

The shape of this rune looks like a little banner or a flag from a string of bunting, and that's exactly how to see it. It's the happiest rune of all; it's party time (you can also remember it as P for party)!

I have personally used this rune on celebration cakes, such as handfasting[4] cakes, where it serves both as a symbol and a charm to

---

4   A pagan wedding ceremony.

bring joy. And don't forget the way the runes speak of sharing and family: so, with Wunjo — it's all about weddings, birthday parties, baby showers, engagements, housewarmings. It can be just about happiness, being contented and having no stresses, enough money and good health and a good relationship. Or it could be some other kind of good news, like the fulfilment of motherhood, success in exams leading to a glittering future career, a medical diagnosis of a condition cleared, promotion at work, etc. Other runes nearby, if you are doing a cast of more than one, will show you what these might be. But it is telling you there are good times ahead.

Wunjo is number eight in the Futhark alphabet, and this brings to mind the eight Sabbats, including Yule, which the Norsemen celebrated just as we do Christmas, with roaring fires, singing and dancing, lots to eat and drink, gifts and parties. Or it could mean a more nationwide event such as the Queen's Jubilee, something that brings people, families and communities together, with all quarrels and bad feelings forgotten and only happiness and goodwill in the air. It speaks of the arrival of a piece of good news — or of a significant date — and the period of peace and happiness that will follow as a result. The deepening of relationships and happiness of families can be implied by this rune, and the growth not only of romantic but intellectual friendships — 'great minds think alike,' as we say.

I feel myself that it can speak of spiritual joy, of the rarely achieved state of grace of which mystics speak, or simply of the joy felt in serving your Gods and being able occasionally to sense their presence and hopefully their approval. There is joy to be had at both church services and pagan rituals, especially when Covid has prevented them for a long time, and in the company of like-minded friends. That is a meaning I can personally align with, the joy I have found in my coven and the pagan friends I have made.

Wishes that come true are included in the meanings of Wunjo, so that it can also be used in magic to bring about greatly desired outcomes, or just carried as a charm to attract happiness.

Murkstave: reversed, Wunjo speaks of a blockage to joy, which could even be self-imposed. Old Ebenezer Scrooge keeps popping into my head as I write about the runes. He was the sort of person the Norsemen would have found utterly pitiful on several levels, and they would have loved Dickens's story and probably understood it just as we do. Wunjo as a murkstave can warn you of pride, prejudice or unreasoning antipathy keeping you from something wonderful which would bring you joy. It is surprising how often we hug our own pride or preconceptions to us as more important to us than genuine happiness. You see it in children, sulking in their rooms rather than coming to make up a quarrel and play; unfortunately, you also see it in adults as well. Wunjo tells you: reach out! Be positive! Be open to happiness. I would add to that: give in to the joy that opening yourself totally to the will of the Gods brings.

Leif: Yule is here! Party time!
Jayden: Christmas is coming… and Yule!

AETT TWO

The rulership of the second Aett is under dispute. Some sources give an almost unknown weather deity called Hagal as the ruler; some will give Hel, and some Heimdallr. Certainly, the second Aett includes a lot of natural occurrences: hail, ice, harvest, sunshine, death. I am going to stick my neck out here and give Hel as the ruler of the middle Aett.

HAGALAZ (H) disruption, shock

PRONOUNCE HAG-al-az
ASSOCIATIONS Hel

This word means hail. You are getting all ready to go on a long-awaited picnic with your friends; the basket is full of sarnies, crisps, home-made traybake and bottles of soda, with some plastic plates tucked down the side. You step out of the door and... Whoosh! Hailstones the size of walnuts are thudding all over, forcing you back into the house, cursing, to text your friends and explain that the treat is off. Not a darned thing you can do about it. So, you take the food you have made and eat it in front of the telly or YouTube, or over a good book, and despite the disappointment, you actually have a nice time anyway.

Hail is a pretty destructive form of weather; big hailstones can break windows, hurt people, batter down crops and garden flowers. Yet, when they have passed, they leave clean, pure water, which will refresh those crops. So, although this looks a lot like Thurisaz from the last Aett, it is different. Actually, many of the runes seem to overlap in this way: alike but not the same; perhaps a kind of spiritual insurance to see you get the right message, whichever runes you draw. Hagalaz can share with Uruz the concept of transformation through suffering but is more likely to mean an unexpected event rather than a danger or pain faced deliberately for the sake of progress. Remember that in pagan belief, both creation and destruction are a vital part of the workings of the Universe: without destruction there cannot be creation, without death there can be no life.

This is the rune that says something important to you is planned, but fate thinks otherwise and there is absolutely nothing you can do about it. It's a sudden calamity interfering with your plans that can leave you raging impotently. You are on your way to a job interview or a date with a potential lover you've met online... and your car breaks down. All you can do is shrug, try to relax and carry on until the problem sorts itself out – no good banging your head against the car bonnet, no matter how much you feel like doing this. And the rune also carries the meaning that all will be well in the end... perhaps the job wasn't all it was cracked up to be, perhaps the Tinder date had bad breath and actually wasn't really your type at all. All you can do is trust in the message and know that your reaction to the sudden calamity will help or hinder your own personal development. Here is an opportunity to rise above the slings and arrows of outrageous fortune and become a more balanced, wiser, calmer person; to become, if you like, more philosophical. It is an opportunity to find the strength within yourself.

I remember when we had young children and one income, and we were going on holiday with spending money carefully hoarded from our slender resources. This vanished overnight when HMRC suddenly stuck their hand out, demanding immediate payment... as they do (we still got the holiday, but it was all sandwiches on the beach!). A good example of Hagalaz. And yes... we had a lovely time, notwithstanding, and our financial situation improved slightly afterwards.

Many sources point out that Hagalaz is the ninth rune, and that nine is a very special and magical number in Norse belief, so this rune becomes 'exalted' – as in astrology. Its shape is easy to remember: just like our own H, H for Hel or hail, or for 'Halt!' – as it is about being brought up short by forces stronger than yourself. The 'H' form of the rune is the older one; the doubled cross-stroke was introduced later.

There is no **murkstave** for this rune.

*Leif: My best cow got out and was lost, a terrible misfortune. But she came
back – and she's pregnant!*

*Jayden: I dropped my smartphone and broke it, just when I needed it the
most. But the insurance covered it and actually bought me an upgrade.*

NAUTHIZ (N) need, hardship, sorrow, slavery

PRONOUNCE NOW-thiz

ASSOCIATIONS the Norns, Loki

Nauthiz, sometimes appearing as Naudhiz with a D, translates as 'need' and is all about hardship and the needs of the body, mind and soul. This quirky rune looks oddly unbalanced, but it is a rough diagram of an ancient bow-drill, a wooden device for spinning a stick in a hole in a log until it catches fire. In a freezing Scandinavian winter, this would have been a need indeed! To people raised in a Christian culture, it looks a bit like crossed fingers: remember, at the time the runes were in use for magic and divination, Christianity was already taking hold in Western Europe. The crossed fingers image is a useful way to remember this rune and its meaning.

We all have needs, daily needs like food, shelter, clothing, an income, love. But the appearance of the rune says that you need these things but do not have them. It can speak of hardship in many guises, from actual hunger to the suffering of a smoker who has just given up, or of hard and unpleasant chores to be got through. The Icelandic rune poem verse for this rune mentions a 'bondmaid', basically a female slave, whose life was no fun most of the time, lots of work and no freedom because of her place in life. She had no rights and, as well as hard work, her position may also have included having to share her owner's bed and bearing his children. So Nauthiz speaks of something in life that cannot be altered, and which causes discomfort, sorrow, hardship. Perhaps this is poverty or a lack of education, homelessness or ill health. Either way, it is something to be endured, something beyond your control.

Well, you probably know about your needs, or you think you do. But Nauthiz draws your attention to deeper needs too, perhaps the need for chill-out time, for time to yourself, time with the Gods, away from the demands of others, time to heal and rest. This rune can often appear for those who are weighed down with work, who carry the world on their shoulders and accept more and more demands because they have never learned to say 'no' (I am a sufferer from Nodding Dog Syndrome, so I know how bad this can get). Well, heed it when it appears and go a bit easier on yourself; you have needs too. It could save you from mega stress and high blood pressure.

Nauthiz can be about the sort of mental chains that slow us all down: guilt, worry, depression, lack of confidence (that's a biggie for most people), anger and other mental problems that can sour your life and pull you down. Another is the need for love, and I've heard this rune will be turned up more frequently by people who are still seeking their life partner. Love itself can cause miserable, painful need, especially if it's one-sided, and the rune can announce the appearance of a person for whom you will have those feelings.

Because of its association with slavery, Nauthiz can mean obligations, constraint, bondage in its most ancient sense: perhaps even to do with human trafficking. Or you are prevented from doing something for legal reasons or from the terms of your employment, perhaps you are on probation or the subject of a restraint order. Or you have been invited to go on holiday and would love to go, but the situation at work is such that you just cannot get away. Certainly, it says you are frustrated by a situation you cannot change, and your response to drawing this rune may be, 'Yeah, tell me about it!' Because we're not talking about, 'I need to wash the car' or, 'I need to mow the lawn' here.

It can also be about, not a physical need but something you need more fundamentally. So often our physical needs – cravings for food, for sex, for comfort – and the needs of our egos can cover up the needs of our spirits, so Nauthiz draws your attention to these. Wyrd can throw things in our path which we can only regard with horror. Yet when we have stumbled over them, we often realise they were put there for our own good, our spiritual welfare, and certainly not for the demands of our bodies and our egos.

I have seen the name of this rune translated on websites as 'need-fire', which is culturally incorrect. The need-fire was a Celtic custom and was lighted in times when purification was needed, such as plagues, when cattle might be driven through the smoke and flames in an attempt to purify them of the murrain. Yet, you can see that this meaning, of a need for help, a need for cleansing in dire times, could also be assigned to Nauthiz.

There is no **murkstave** for this rune as it is not reversible, but the rune does nevertheless have a reverse side: it can also speak of the absence of need, and the fact that this too can be a negative situation, difficult as that may be to understand. I always think the maxim, 'All work and no play make Jack a dull boy' has it the wrong way round. We need to work; we need to need. The child of rich and overindulgent parents, who knows no need, is not likely to be happy or to grow up well-balanced and contented, nor compassionate towards others less fortunate. The cliché of the 'we was poor but we was 'appy' home life holds a profound truth.

Leif: The lowest part of the winter; we have hardly enough to eat.
Jayden: Amber's been on Depop again – we're broke!

ISA (I) freeze

PRONOUNCE EES-a
ASSOCIATIONS the Norn Verdandi and Skadi

This simple rune looks like an icicle – and ice is just what it means: you're frozen! You're stuck in metaphorical ice and cannot move forward.

I thought of this rune a lot when the first Covid lockdown came into force in 2020, as it was very relevant to that situation. Here we all were, stuck in our homes, unable to get out or to get on with anything, unable to progress plans, not even able to go and see friends or family. Isa shares with Hagalaz the idea of plans being frustrated, but it is in a very different way. Where Hagalaz is sudden disaster, Isa is a simple shutdown of all action through natural causes and happening, as it were, overnight with no violence and no shock – just as you can wake up to find snow has fallen and it is impossible to get to where you want to go. Unlike Hagalaz, Isa can even indicate a situation that was expected – like bad weather. There can be something beautiful about the process, just as ice is beautiful in its glistening white purity. I think we all felt at the time that the lockdown was not all bad: many of us enjoyed an unscheduled holiday from work and from many of our responsibilities, and stayed peacefully at home, enjoying domestic comfort, perhaps catching up on DIY, or our reading or our hobbies. It took a few weeks for real frustration to set in.

Your frustrating blockage may be due to any cause: lack of money, poor health, the 'glass ceiling' that women and people of ethnic minority backgrounds may suffer in their careers, being stuck in a particular place for family reasons – perhaps you need to move for your work, but the children are in their last year at school, or if you are older, your parents are perhaps becoming dependent and need you there.

Moving deeper into the rune, the freeze may be down to longstanding emotional situations, such as a grievance or a longstanding quarrel, or some other kind of psychological blockage. For years, I thought I was rubbish at knitting because my mother – not the most patient person – taught me and was always throwing up her hands in horror at the work I did. It took me years to get past this and discover that I was actually quite good at knitting and could even write my own patterns – I still don't like it though! You'll often hear someone say, 'Oh, I'm no good at that sort of thing'. Maybe they've never really tried, and this idea might go right back to their childhood, and some unkind person sneering at their early attempts. These things stick and become self-fulfilling prophecies that are extremely hard to shift. People make all sorts of excuses for not doing things that scare them, such as, 'It's not the right time' or, 'I'm too busy right now'.

Isa can also speak of attitudes frozen in time, perhaps based on first impressions or old prejudices from our youth which should have gone into the mental recycle bin a long time ago but have never been taken out and looked at properly. Isa can bring our attention to these sorts of self-imposed limitations and help us to get past them.

Ice can be a trap. Whilst I think other runes might be more likely to indicate actual danger, Isa does carry this meaning of being 'stuck in the ice' or trapped by circumstances, and these can include the state of being stuck in a job you hate but need financially, or a loveless relationship arising perhaps out of an unplanned pregnancy, or even the warning that such a situation might arise if you are not careful. Many of us perhaps know people trapped in a bad marriage for reasons other than love: the threat of violence or self-harm, the children (who would probably be better off with one happy parent than two warring ones), even financial circumstances which mean it would be too difficult to break up the home. Isa can also mean literal imprisonment, or enslavement in some other sense, such as addiction to drugs, alcohol or tobacco.

In spiritual terms, this rune speaks of the feeling that comes upon all seekers sooner or later: that they have lost their direct line to the Gods and are all alone in the Universe. It is a feeling that can crush even experienced worshippers and leave them feeling they have perhaps chosen the wrong path or are wasting their time believing in the Gods.

But, as with Hagalaz, Isa melts. It melts and refreshes, and things could be even better afterwards if you can sit out the situation without losing your cool. The ice of the winter melts and spring flowers take its place.

In some books and websites, you will read a lot about this rune being equal to our letter I and thus the pronoun I, and therefore being to do with ego. This is an interesting idea, but wrong, as the Old Norse pronoun equivalent is *iak*, which as you can see, morphed into pronouns like 'ich' and 'Jeg' in later languages. But you can make your own decisions about information like this, which is not correct but does seem as though it might be onto something.

There is no **murkstave** for this rune, but Isa does emphasise runes that fall around it or touch it, strengthening their meaning.

Leif: Over in the little valley further along the coast is a great deal of fertile land ready for the plough. But I can't leave home with Frida heavy with child and three of my cows about to calve.

Jayden: I would so love to accept that Manchester job, what a step up, but Amber won't leave London.

JERA (J or Y) harvest

PRONOUNCE YAIR-a
ASSOCIATIONS Freyr

This word, which in Old Norse means 'harvest', comes from the same root as our word 'year' and can also denote a calendar year. It is associated with the pagan 'harvest' Sabbats of Lammas (around 1st August) and Mabon (autumn equinox), and also with the two solstices. In other words, it speaks of a full year, but with the emphasis on the end of the grain cycle. It's the only rune to be made up from two separate pieces — which look a bit like two sickles or scythes working towards one another across a field, which is a good image and a useful way to remember it.

Jera, like all the runes associated with Freyr, is a very positive one, speaking of rewards and harvests, fruition of plans, hard work paying off, perhaps a financial plan maturing. We don't need to be Dark Ages farmers gathering in crops before the weather closes in to understand this concept. Something you have earned is coming your way — in a good way.

Apart from the odd row of garden herbs and runner beans in the back garden, none of us is especially concerned with the harvest of actual crops, so how does this rune speak to us?

It actually has quite a lot in common with Uruz... but hold the pain and fear. Everyone understands what harvest means: all your hard work has paid off and here comes your reward! The kinds of things that Jera may be speaking of to a 21st century practitioner may include a financial payoff after years of scrimping and saving, a qualification gained after a long period of study, a promotion at work after a long time spent learning the job, the completion of a fixer-up house which you can then sell for a large profit. It could speak of a well-earned and saved-for retirement, or a resolution in a long-running legal case. As this is a fertility rune, it could even refer to a more personal harvest, perhaps that of a pregnancy after months of trying, even after IVF.

However, Jera is not really about a one-off event; it speaks of cycles (not the wheeled kind). The barley is gathered in, but it doesn't just feed the tribe for the winter; it also provides the seed corn for the following year, and so it goes on. And of course, being a Norse oracle, it implies a community festivity rather than an individual one – those wonderful harvest home suppers in 19th century novels by people like Thomas Hardy come to mind, at which all, regardless of status, get together for a good old knees-up with plenty to eat and drink. If Jera speaks to you, it probably means the good news is for your family – your tribe – as a whole.

To modern eyes, this rune looks like a logo for a brand of car or some other fast-moving apparatus. Yet it speaks not of speed, but of slowness and deliberation, of waiting, work and planning. It says time must pass before rewards are reaped, and it counsels patience. It also speaks of choosing the right time and of time moving on, whether you want it to or not. 'This too shall pass,' it says. Expressions like this, that we think of as typically modern and English, may go back generations and into other cultures, or echo similar expressions that were used in other civilisations.

Jera speaks of the cyclical nature of life, something of which we pagans are particularly aware, and can even speak of death, though not in an ominous way. If you have experienced a bereavement and draw this rune, it is telling you that grief will not go on forever, that death is the way of things and the natural end of life, and that even this separation will not be forever. Accept the course of life, go with the flow. Take the rough with the smooth, as it is all part of the dance of life. The cold rain, as well as the warm sun, are both necessary to make us what we need to be.

There is no **murkstave** for this rune. However, like all the runes, it can be coloured by runes nearby and can have a shadow side. In this case, it could mean someone getting their just rewards in a less positive way: perhaps someone who has been unkind to you for a long time gets what is coming to them. But I feel this would be more a function of Teiwaz, the first rune of the last Aett.

Leif: Harvest time!
Jayden: Cool, my MCSE qualification came through.

EIWAZ (I or AI, like the vowel sound in 'sigh') endings and beginnings

PRONOUNCE EYE-waz
ASSOCIATIONS Odin and Hel

Sometimes *Eihwaz* or *Ihwaz*, this is the 13th rune and corresponds to the Death card in Tarot, which is also the 13th.

Here we have another rune that is easily confused with others. Its name is very similar to Ehwaz, and its shape to that of Sowelu. Having a mental picture to go with the runes is always helpful, and in this case, I remember the word 'scythe' – not only the implement Death carries, but the vowel sound is the same. If you see the rune stave itself as a scythe with a 'foot' on it, that will also help. The rune is said to represent a yew tree, and ancient yews are very prone to drooping their branches in the manner of the top stroke of the symbol.

The yew is deeply associated with death in our minds for several reasons, from its use in making the longbow, which was the deadliest weapon at Agincourt, the equivalent then of a heat-seeking missile. The tree's rather dark and forbidding appearance and the custom of planting yew trees in churchyards to keep farmers from grazing their livestock there has reinforced this association. It was deeply associated in Norse and Celtic belief with the underworld (in the tree oracle, Ogham the yew, Idho, also means a dramatic change, an ending and even death) and the cult of the dead, and people of those times also planted yew trees at their burial sites. As many of these sites were later used for Christian churches, the yew trees may often be older than the church itself. Just to reinforce this association, many parts of the tree are also quite poisonous.

So, do we start to tremble when we see this rune turn up, and start looking at funeral plans? No, of course not, any more than a Tarot reader turning up the Death card. Yes, it can speak of endings, but the message is given very well by the yew tree's habit of regeneration. These amazing trees may come crashing down in a storm, but they carry on, sending up new shoots from their prone position, and pretty much living forever. The National Trust has a specimen at Ankerwycke in Surrey that is believed to be...wait for it...two and a half *millennia* old.

This tree is as deeply associated with life and regeneration as it is with death: its longevity and resistance to disease and storms, and the modern use of its chemical components to fight cancer; even the use of its wood to make bows can be seen as *giving* life, when you consider their use to provide meat for people in the past, as well as defending them from attackers. As an evergreen, it changes its appearance very little from year to year, and so becomes an obvious symbol of eternity and everlasting life, life beyond death. It indicates the womb as well as the grave.

Eiwaz is about endings and beginnings, doorways and thresholds, eternity and regeneration. *Something is coming to an end*, says Eiwaz, *something in your life will change drastically*. But this could just as easily be something positive as negative. It does not specifically state that this will be negative, let alone that you or anyone close to you will die. It could just as easily mean your elderly laptop will die and you will have to get a new one, or your job contract expires, and you are given a new job. Something in your life has been outgrown and will need to be discarded for a new one, a change that might not have happened by itself because of laziness, fear or inertia — we don't like change much, most of us, but sometimes it is vital.

Take the rune with trust and try not to let its taint of death colour its meaning with fear. As with all the runes, trust the Gods to know what is best, and that changes brought about by Wyrd[5] are always in your best or highest interests. You can even carry the rune as a charm to aid personal transformation. See? Not scary at all.

There is no **murkstave** for this rune.

Leif: The old Earl is dead....What will life under his son be like?
Jayden: My boss is moving on. Three years I've put up with that bastard,
but now I'll have a new manager.

PERTHO (P) chance, fate, mystery

PRONOUNCE PAIR-tho
ASSOCIATIONS The Norns and Frigga

Sometimes Perthro or Peorth, this rune replaces the blank rune sometimes found in some sets, which really has no business being

---

5   Fate — see Chapter Three.

there. The undisputed meaning of this rune has been lost, and it is only possible to hazard a guess based on its shape and the rune poems' cryptic words. Scholars have suggested that the rune resembles a dicing cup lying on its side – as though the dice have been thrown – which ties in with the reference to gaming in the poem.

So, we take this rune to represent luck, chance, fate, *Wyrd* and *Orlog*[6], or a simple message that what you asked about is in the lap of the Gods, and you will have to wait and see. The rune could also show a cauldron lying on its side, and orlog was represented by a cauldron... your actions in life went into the mix, into the cauldron of orlog and what came out was your just reward, your future fate, dictated by your own choices and behaviour. The rune corresponds to the Wheel of Fortune in the Tarot.

And that is pretty much all there is to say on the meaning of this mysterious rune, but as with all the runes, you will build up a relationship with it and it will give you messages. If you have any problem with the meaning of this rune, I would suggest you dowse the rune with your pendulum and ascertain for the future what meaning this rune has for you.

There is no **murkstave** for this rune, and Leif and Jayden have no answer to their daily question.

---

6   See Chapter Three.

ALGIZ (Z) protection

PRONOUNCE AHL-giz
ASSOCIATIONS Heimdallr, the Valkyries

Sometimes rendered Elhaz, this name is hard to translate, but the prickliest answer seems the most relevant to me. While its shape seems to portray a man standing with his arms out to protect something or someone, the rune is associated with the elk sedge *Cladium mariscus*, a very thorny customer indeed. Farmers in all ages have used thorny plants as hedging to protect their livestock, or even themselves, from harm. Our English words: hedge and edge are from the same root and related to the Anglo-Saxon *hay*, meaning both a boundary and a hedgerow. When you see a picture of the elk sedge you can see it may have inspired the rune's shape, or it could be based on an elk's antlers. Either way, the plant is a vicious thing that knows how to protect itself; having razor-sharp edges that will rip the skin of any hand that takes hold of it. The Norsemen used it for thatching roofs, and you can only hope they equipped themselves with thick leather gloves first. Associated with a roof and with its own weapons, the elk sedge is easy to see as protection, but the easiest way to remember this rune shape is as a person standing with their arms out, to stop someone else being attacked, a good image for Algiz.

The shape of Algiz is one that occurs commonly in nature, so messages involving this rune may appear in hedgerows, twigs, bird formations and in man-made structures.

Algiz is your mother's arms, outspread to snatch you up and comfort you when you have fallen and hurt yourself, or the school bully followed you home from class. Where Christians might make the sign of the Cross, or cross their fingers against harm, the old Germanic races had a protective gesture that involved folding the thumb and pinky finger into the palm of the hand and spreading out the three other fingers like a fork. Warriors would have this symbol on their shields or weapons, to protect them from harm in battle.

When this rune appears upright, it brings the message that you are protected from harm. It can mean the appearance of someone performing any job that protects people, a uniformed person such as a police officer, a soldier, a fireman, or a doctor or medical staff member. However, it does not counsel complacency; its appearance is a sign that you should be on your guard and doing things to protect yourself as well. Now is the time to go round and renew the magical protections on your home and car, to check your firewall is okay, make safety checks and to take care not to put yourself in any danger.

This rune above all is used as an amulet by pagans and rune users, who will hang it around their necks, or over doorways or from the rear-view mirror of their car to keep them and their loved ones from harm. It can also be tied in with other runes to fortify it and specify protection in certain situations, and its shape lends itself to this well.

While the central meaning of Algiz is protection, it also means divine protection, either as an instruction to seek this through prayer and sacrifice or just the knowledge that your patron deity will be there for you, and that you can trust him or her. The ancient pagans typically did not kneel to their Gods, but stood before them with their arms raised, and Algiz also calls this pose to mind. However, as many of us on a spiritual path have found, this doesn't mean you can lie back and relax… the Gods help those who help themselves, and one of the things the Norse valued above all else was courage – which is not the same as the absence of fear. One of the meanings of this rune reversed is that the Gods are pissed with you, and that you know why. Perhaps you have behaved badly to someone else, or been selfish, and now face retribution.

In all human lives come bad situations, sometimes so bad that you feel you cannot face it alone. The Gods are there for you, but they do not expect to simply steer harm away from you, while you play games on your phone. They want you up and fighting by their side, showing willing, and then their blessing and help will come to you.

So, as we can see, the more spiritual meanings of this rune are of the higher self and the connection with deity, the call to prayer and religious duties and the rewards these might bring. It speaks of the respite and protection that prayer and other kinds of communing with the Gods may offer from weltschmerz, the sorrows of the soul. As with Christian beliefs, the Norse Gods can be a refuge: if you are deserving.

Murkstave: this means pretty much the reverse of the above: that you are not protected, the Gods do not have your back, and you had better get up quickly and do something about it. Now is the time to sort out your protection, hang amulets, up your prayer count, sprinkle salt and smudge with sage, because danger is coming, and you must not let it catch you off guard. It is a warning.

Leif: Wolves are about, and the cows and goats are restless. I'll hang Algiz
  runes about the homestead to protect us all.
Jayden: There's a new kind of malware about; I'll update my security and
  protect my set-up with Algiz runes.

SOWELU (S) Sun, completion

PRONOUNCE so-WEL-oo
ASSOCIATIONS Baldr, Sunna

Coming now to the last rune of the second Aett, Sowelu is one of the more familiar runic shapes, due to its unfortunate involvement in the iconography of the Nazi Party, who used it on the armbands, collar patches and other uniform components of the SS. Its shape derives from the Latin-Etruscan letter S, and ultimately from the Greek Sigma. In very early variants, it is sometimes seen as a slightly attenuated Sigma, but the slightly later form is a clear and unmistakable S. The shape is a lightning bolt, fairly different from the 'scythe' of Eiwaz. It could also be doubled and crossed to form the swastika – another Sun symbol appropriated by the Nazis.

The Germanic peoples saw the Sun as feminine and the Goddess thereof was Sunna (the Moon, even more weirdly, was seen as masculine, despite its monthly cycle).

Today we are a little more ambivalent about the Sun, being aware that it can kill as well as comfort, but to the Norsemen, it was nothing but positive. How they must have yearned for it through the long dark northern winters and the endless polar nights, for its light, warmth and benefit to crops. So, the mundane meaning of this rune is all the good things we associate with the Sun: warmth, comfort, light, good health, good fortune, prosperity. The Sun shines on us and everything we do. A divine blessing.

Sowelu is an incredibly positive rune, one of the most positive of all. It casts a favourable light over all the runes in a cast and, best of all, is to find it showing up next to Jera and Wunjo.

The Sun blesses everything it touches, ripening grain and fruit, warming and cheering the people, causing the grass to grow, and thus removing the need for cattle to be penned or slaughtered. It brought to the Norse happiness, abundance and comfort of a quality we in the 21st century, with our central heating and tumble-dryers, can hardly appreciate. Yet even today it still has the same effect on us: even when you're at work all day, if it's hot and sunny it suddenly feels like a holiday; people get into a different mindset, don't they? Nothing seems to matter that much, and everyone is positive. The Sun brings a sense of completeness and content.

Anyone with a little knowledge of astrology and Correspondences (a body of knowledge used by witches that ties together astrology, herbs, crystals, colours and other elements) can take that a step further and start to bring in influences such as the traits of Leo, which speak of leadership, charm, generosity, artistic creativity, enthusiasm, courage and confidence: the sort of person who will walk into anywhere as though they owned the place – and probably be treated as though they do. The Sun rules joy, pride, success, prosperity, promotion, leadership and advancement, as well as the arts, especially music and poetry, and healing. It is the planet of kings.

Sunshine heals: it creates substances in the body that are vital for our wellbeing, such as melatonin, without which we become depressed and cannot sleep, and also vitamin D, vital for the immune system and for the growth and maintenance of bones and teeth – without it children and adults can develop rickets. It dries up wounds and rashes and stimulates hair growth.

Moving on from its mundane meanings, Sowelu speaks of the inner self and the higher self, and the oldest rune poem says of it: the Sun guides seafarers. Is this not a hint that Sowelu might also guide us on our karmic journey, pointing the way to go in a runecast? Throughout the cultures of the past, the Sun has been honoured as the chiefest of divinities, from Japan and Ancient Egypt to Ireland and the Americas.

The Sun is also the source of light, both the light to see and read and work, but also the light of truth and revelation, the light that heals and cleans, as when the sunlight hits the slimy mess revealed when a rock is turned over. Truth can also bring understanding, and so forgiveness and acceptance. It banishes darkness and ignorance, thaws the frozen heart and heals grief, loneliness and sorrow.

The wheel has long been associated with the Sun across many cultures, who either saw the disc as a divine chariot or as an actual wheel. So, the rune also speaks of progress and gives the advice that while success is assured, one must then move on. Speaking of a person, it may indicate a traveller or someone with a playful, adventurous nature, or even a young child.

There is no murkstave for Sowelu, and it is difficult to see how this rune could contain any negative energies, but you can sometimes see very extreme positives as not desirable: for example, the tendency towards arrogance and even bossiness of people with a Leo sun-sign. But light and warmth may have their drawbacks too, as when you have got too comfortable by the fire and then it is so much more difficult when you must get up and go out in the cold for something important.

Magically, Sowelu is made for charms for good fortune, and its shape also fits snugly with other runes. Here it is in a good luck bindrune with Jera, the harvest rune.

Leif: All I have touched today has turned to gold; a blessed day!
Jayden: You know what? I just feel bloody brilliant today!

AETT THREE

The God Tyr rules the third Aett, in which the runes are largely about human behaviour and relationships, and his own rune Teiwaz is the first in this Aett.

TEIWAZ (T) justice, honour, sacrifice, revenge

PRONOUNCE TYE-waz
ASSOCIATIONS Tyr — Sometimes Tiwaz

Coming now to the last of the three Aetts, we start with a rune that is deeply identified with the God after whom the Aett is named. The ancient War God Tyr or Tiw was perhaps once a pantheon head, and a creator God in early belief, but later a God of Justice, War and Battle who aligns with Aries or Mars and gives his name to the day Tuesday. The Aett starts with Teiwaz, which is appropriately shaped like an arrow or spear — an easy way to remember this rune and its war God patron.

Tyr himself translates to Sir Galahad in British mythological terms, a white knight figure of honour and truth. He made a terrible sacrifice for the good of all, losing his right hand — and without anaesthetic — for the safety of the tribe (something the Norse would have considered the ultimate good deed).

The message from this rune, drawn singly, is one of hope, that all will be well if you act with integrity and have nothing to be ashamed of. Teiwaz is a rune of justice, and of some rather old-fashioned sounding virtues like truth, integrity, honour, purity and righteousness — for those of us who know the Egyptian pantheon, it corresponds to the deified concept of Ma'at. Speak the truth and shame the Devil, says this rune. In paganism, we sometimes speak of 'standing in our own space and speaking our own truth'. Tyr and Teiwaz smile on those who speak the truth, keep their promises, are loyal to their fellow soldiers and show courage in the face of battle. This is NOT a rune of mindless violence, though it may indicate that a struggle is before you. Fight the good fight, says the rune.

Teiwaz is about courage, and especially the courage to do the right thing, which as we all know, is often easier to think about than do. Teiwaz promises victory, if your cause be just, but to beware if you are dishonourable, vindictive or lacking in compassion. The person who will benefit from this rune is one who carries all the qualities it speaks of. To someone who has already come to grief through their own dishonourable, spiteful or selfish behaviour it says, 'Serves you right.'

Teiwaz can mean an actual person, someone with these great and good qualities, arriving to save your bacon, a real white knight. Perhaps a friend or relative turning up to save you when you are in trouble or at a low ebb, or even a professional — many of us have felt this way about the AA man when we have been left stranded on the hard shoulder by a breakdown. Or paramedics, true heroes in anyone's book, arriving on the scene of a catastrophe to bring help and relief. It could even mean you, who drew the rune, telling you that you may need to assume this mantle and go to the aid of another person, like the hero you are at heart!

Tyr was associated with priesthood, so the rune may indicate a man or woman of the Cloth, or it could be telling you that your spiritual mentor has arrived, someone who will be your guide and support you on your path. Or in the mundane world, a friend who serves in the same role — we all have people in our lives who have moulded us, taught us about eternal verities, changed us in some way — especially when we were younger.

Another important aspect of this rune is the reason for Tyr's sacrifice: as Star Trek's Mr Spock says, 'The needs of the many outweigh the needs of the few', and Tyr acts to his own detriment for the sake of the other Gods and creatures in the Norse world. To the Norse, this self-sacrifice for the sake of the common good would strike a very deep chord. This is the hero who sacrifices himself for a higher cause, who puts himself in danger for his ideals or to protect others. He is also incredibly cool about it: as a child I was very struck with the tale of the bound wolf, and the rejoicing of the Gods when Fenris was chained. Only Tyr did not rejoice, for he had lost his hand — which seemed to be his only reaction to this calamity, all very Spartan. The rune is closely associated with the North Star and its stationary guiding role in the sky. Tyr brings order when all has been chaos: just as he, the God of Justice, quelled the wolf son of Chaos with his courage. So, the rune also speaks of calm and courage together, and of setting this example to others and using it to reduce panic in others.

The other side of this rune is about the rewards of dishonourable behaviour, of someone getting what is coming to them, perhaps a physical wound caused by their own bad behaviour, or some other form of comeuppance.

Magically, this rune can be used as a talisman in situations where justice is being sought — provided the cause is truly just and will not cause undeserved harm to anyone. The Norse carried the rune in to battle as a charm, believing it would help them win and avoid injury.

Murkstave: you will get your due punishment for your bad or dishonourable or cruel behaviour to another. Do not try to use force or aggression in a situation; it is not the answer. Find an alternative way. And be sure your own conscience is clear before you start crying for justice.

Leif: My neighbour's best milk cow has wandered onto my land. I could keep her, but that would be dishonourable.
Jayden: Amber's hot friend came onto me; but I'm not that kind of guy.

BERKANA (B) new beginnings, nurturing

PRONOUNCE BAIR-ka-na
ASSOCIATIONS Nerthus, Frigga and Freyja

Berkana (sometimes Berkano) is one of the runes that clearly shows its ancestry of our own corresponding letter, which is B, so it is easily remembered as B for birth, B for beginnings. The shape of the rune is said to be based on a woman's breasts, which is a useful way of remembering this nurturing rune, and the word Berkana means birch twig. This beautiful tree has long been regarded as feminine and maternal – the Druids call it The Lady of the Woods, and in the Ogham, Beith represents new beginnings.

The most obvious meaning of this rune is birth, so new beginnings, and the act of nurturing. You can see this rune as representing the Goddess in all Her creative glory, She who made the world and is mother to every creature in it. The rune speaks of female power and of traditionally female concerns such as the nurturing of children. It can also represent feminine beauty – the tree itself is a very graceful, slight tree with very motile leaves that seem to glitter in the sunlight, and of course it has that amazing silvery white trunk and boughs. Berkana can also be about secrecy, as the secrecy of the unborn child not yet visible as it grows in the womb. Down the ages, women have concealed their pregnancies for a variety of reasons; even today with a woman who is delighted to be pregnant, there is still the sense of a secret, and the awaiting of the right time to 'tell everyone her news'. It speaks of secrecy in a very positive sense, not one of deceit, but of care and protection. The tree speaks of safety and particularly safety through secrecy, and the usefulness of secrecy in all sorts of situations: we might think of the magical elemental mantra, *to know, to dare, to will and to keep silent*. Because it speaks of female power, the rune also carries the meanings of female maturity and the virtues thereof: wisdom, patience, compassion and the practical abilities of women who have perhaps cared for a home and family for many years, and possibly even the inherited wisdom that goes with this, which in the past travelled down many generations.

So, you can see that the rune can also refer to all kinds of supportive relationships, and not just with women or girls, but also to supportive males, all friends who care and are likely to be there for you when you need them.

Berkana is strongly connected with healing, and is certainly a rune to be used in conjunction with other runes and other work to promote healing. If Britain were a pagan country, we might well expect to find the Berkana symbol on the front of hospitals! Certainly, one of the figures it evokes is that of a trained nurse, competent, practical and caring, although it can also represent any type of healthcare professional or anyone who is offering healing of any kind.

Berkana can mean pregnancy and fertility, especially if Ingwaz or Othila – the runes of sex and family – are nearby, but more typically it is about beginning a new project, and it tells you to go ahead and let your ideas bear fruit and be open to new ideas as well. The birch tree is also one that will regrow suckers from its roots if the main trunk is damaged, and the rune also speaks of rebirth and regeneration, of sweeping away dead wood to let new ideas grow through. Like Eiwaz the yew, the birch tree perseveres and is not easily destroyed. The rune was also used to ease childbirth.

The Norse witches used this rune a lot in their magical practices, as they did the tree itself. The birch was sacred to the Goddess Bercha or Bertha, an aspect of the Earth Goddess, and birch was used for wands which were used for purification – just as we might use the scourge in modern Wicca. Young men were ritually beaten with birch twigs. This practice, which we might tend to associate nowadays with perverse Edwardian schoolteachers, had a completely different meaning for the Norse; it was intended to stimulate their health and fertility, their manhood and strength. Even today, beating with birch twigs is seen as a pleasurable and stimulating part of the sauna experience in some countries.

On a spiritual level, the rune speaks of women's mysteries and initiation and is thus a very meaningful rune for Wicca with its high priestesses and predominantly female covens. Again, the secrecy meaning of Berkana is relevant, and traditional in Wicca, where members are adjured not to 'out' their co-religionists.

Murkstave: the mundane meaning is a lack of fertility, such as with a couple trying to conceive. The reversed rune may also speak of new beginnings, but in a negative way. Now is not the time, the conditions are not right, there are difficulties in the way. It could mean aborted plans or difficult beginnings. The secrecy aspect of this rune may indicate secrecy in a more negative way when reversed, as a secret being kept from you, deceit being practised.

Leif: I watch my wife Frida with the children, and the new baby, and know I chose well.

Jayden: Finished work, tired and fed up with a splitting headache. My Amber was there for me with a cold beer and a neck rub.

EHWAZ (E, as in obey) work, partnership, co-operation

PRONOUNCE AY-waz
ASSOCIATIONS Odin and Sleipnir

The easiest image for this rune is two horses' heads turning trustingly toward one another as they work together to pull a heavy load. But let us forget for a moment that this rune is based on horses, for horses don't play a very big part in our lives in the 21st century. The rune is not about stables and bridles and hay, it's about the concepts that were represented to the Norsemen by these things. Where Raido is about the act of riding and the journey, Ehwaz is more clearly based on the means of progress: the horses. Or, as they might translate into modern terms, the mechanics and the partnership of work and motion. It is about two or more people working together towards a common goal. In modern times it is more likely to refer to a married couple working to buy their first home, or two guys who have just started their own business and are working all the hours God sends, or two people who have not liked each other in the past but have agreed to set aside their differences and work together for their common good.

Because we are reading the runes now in this age, it can also speak of modern machines used for transport, and working vehicles, perhaps machinery of all types. Equally important as the horse to this rune is the concept of harness, with all that implies. I have seen it suggested that the shape of the rune is based on a horse's bit. The image that goes with Ehwaz is of two horses harnessed to a wagon and giving their best, working together, using their strength and also, importantly, their experience of and their trust for one another to pull the load. This rune is also associated with human partnerships, business and work partnerships: several of the runes speak of movement and progress, but this one has the particular meaning of progress through teamwork, of people working together having more success than one struggling on alone. It can also mean the emotions that go with this: loyalty, trust, dependence, harmony, respect, understanding and friendship or even love.

It can speak of the experience of learning about ourselves from others, or of a lifelong friendship.

Okay, let's let the animals back in, because this rune is more strongly connected with them than many of the others. Whilst it can certainly mean travel involving horses, it can also speak of animals in general and the relationship with them, and particularly working animals: horses, farm dogs, support dogs. There is also the relationship of the horse and the rider, which I am told can be very deep and complex, almost like a human marriage. This co-operation, of horse and man, of horse and horse, or of person and person, is what produces the result, the attainment of goals. The Norsemen saw the horse as a magical and special animal (as indeed it is) and used Ehwaz magically as a rune of good fortune. It can also be used to protect horses; and aligns with the magical eight-legged horse owned by Odin called Sleipnir (see next chapter).

When reading the oracles of a past culture, I personally feel it is fine to add to the inherited messages an overlay of our own cultural nuances, providing they do not contradict the original meanings. Just to give a few examples: a workhorse, a willing horse, automotive horsepower, in IT 'intel thoroughbreds'. What does the horse conjure up for you? Sometimes the little flash of meaning you get when you first turn over a Tarot card or rune is quite important, maybe more so than the official given meaning of the rune according to books.

Because it is about travel and progress, Ehwaz can also mean a move from one place to another or a change in your life such as a promotion or relocation in your job. It can mean the love of travel for its own sake, or a person who demonstrates this quality.

Finally, the rune is associated with boundaries and land ownership. Because of the Norsemen's lack of drones and theodolites, in the days when the Land Registry Office was not yet in existence, land was often measured in terms of the distance a horse rider could travel in a certain amount of time. This can include the meaning of boundaries of different kinds, including self-imposed ones.

Murkstave: reversed, the rune points to a lack of motivation in a partnership, or an inability to work 'in harness' with someone else, and the lack of progress this will bring. It can mean a lack of trust or the breakdown of a relationship or partnership.

Leif: I took old Svartfaxi out to plough the western field today. He hardly needs a touch on the harness; it's as though he reads my mind.
Jayden: The girlfriend and I have decided to buy a bigger flat together; it will mean a lot of scrimping and saving, but we're up for that.

MANNAZ (M) humanity, the self, mind and thought

PRONOUNCE as it appears
ASSOCIATIONS Heimdallr, Huginn and Munin

This rune is quite challenging to understand. Some methods of divination call for a single stone or tile to be laid down first, representing the person asking for advice, and it has been suggested that Mannaz could be used in this way. Its shape could be that of two people leaning very closely together (no social distancing at all) to talk in private, though it could also be a person examining themselves very closely in the mirror. These are both excellent mnemonic images for this rune, which is about the self and how the self relates to others.

Learning the meaning of this rune will take some thought, as its meaning is quite vague, but I feel that it is to do with humanity: it is you and it is everyone. It is about self and the soul's journey, and has something to do with my own belief that we are 'not as separate as we like to think we are', that it is about common human experience and the human condition and our connection with one another, about normal human thought processes.

Perhaps an easy way of thinking of it is that shared experience we all have, of being aware of our own existence in early childhood, and then, as we grow up, developing metacognition, realising that this same spark is in everyone – we are all the same.

It can also mean the collective potential, and presumably also the negative potential for a race that has brought its home planet to the verge of catastrophe through its selfishness and thoughtlessness.

Mannaz speaks of the individual and the race, the knowledge that some of us have that some persons are awakened, some are enlightened and some slumber on through life, all are at different places on their path. It speaks of the vanity of the ego (as the rune poem remarks, everybody, every *body* is cast aside into the dust at the end of life, and only the spirit goes on). This rune shares the task of the servant, placed in the general's chariot as he led the procession of his triumph through ancient Rome, his purpose being to continually whisper in the general's ear, 'Memento mori' — *remember you are mortal*. Mannaz calls for humility in the face of the Gods, of Wyrd and Orlog, which no person can escape. It speaks of mortality.

On a more mundane level, it speaks of people, of the love they have for one another, of the importance of family and friends, of the *tribe*, and the loneliness and misery we would experience without this support. It is about the preciousness of people close to us and the pleasure we get from normal human interaction, just as the murkstave speaks of loneliness, of farewells, quarrels and alienation from one's fellow man. This rune says, 'No man is an island', and lets us know that everything we experience has been experienced before by others and will be again. We are all fellow travellers on the Way of Wyrd, and should reach out to one another, overcoming racial barriers, prejudice and arrogance.

Mannaz also speaks of the amazing human mind, of its greed for knowledge and its abilities for memory and understanding, of the miracle of human consciousness. It is about curiosity and other human gifts. It is our collective memories, our race memories, our instinctive wisdom, born out of generations of past ancestors. Only in the last few decades has the wisdom of the past and of older people been so generally despised, which is our loss. Scientific 'progress' has often meant throwing aside other knowledge which is just as important.

Because it is tied so firmly to the concept of mind; of intelligence, thought and memory, the rune can be used magically in any situation where help is needed with thought and memory, perhaps an exam. But it also says, 'know yourself', know your own strengths and weaknesses, and be stronger as a result. And knowing yourself, you can be there for others when they are going through things you have experienced yourself.

Mannaz may indicate the influence of a community, especially a spiritual community of some sort, those with whom your soul is more closely aligned. It says, step back and see the bigger picture, of how others are coping, rather than just oneself.

Murkstave: hatred, quarrels and farewells, isolation, loneliness and bitterness.

Leif: My memories of my father are precious to me; all his advice stays with me for when times are hard.

Jayden: I look at Amber sometimes, and wonder what's going on in there. Amazing to think this other person, so different and so much her own person, is mine.

LAGUZ (L) water, birth and rebirth

PRONOUNCE LAG-ooz
ASSOCIATIONS Njörd

I see this rune as the head of 'Nessie', as shown in the infamous Surgeon's photograph, or other water monster. The Norsemen certainly believed in these mythical beasts, and who are we to smile at them for that? There are more tourists visiting Inverness than ever went there for the scenery or the haggis sandwiches.

We are moving into deep waters with this rune, the name of which has a common root with our words 'lake' and 'lagoon' but seems to mean 'leek' (and not 'leak'!). But it also evokes the mysteries of deep waters, both actual and spiritual.

Water is deeply connected with both birth and death. Physical birth involves a great deal of water, from the waters of the womb to the traditional boiling water called for in birth situations in corny old films. The Norse sprinkled their new-born children with water in a ritual similar to a Christian baptism. In the same way, water may be connected with death, from the traditional washing which was part of the laying out of the dead to the still current burial at sea or in water; to this day the Hindus commit the ashes of their dead to the Ganges. The Norse believed – in common with many ancient peoples – that after death the soul journeyed across water to reach the other world, which is why they went in for burials on boats and ships which were set on fire and pushed out onto the water or buried in a tumulus.

In the neopagan tradition, water stands for the emotions, imagination, intuition and the astral part of the soul, for inspiration, divine or artistic, for poetry and music, all that comes from the creative side of man. It also stands for the unconscious and dreams. We place this element in the West, the direction we associate with death and the afterlife. In Wicca, we also associate water with initiation; we address the western element Lords, the spirits of water, as 'ye lords of death and initiation', and blessed water is used in the rite of initiation at First Degree. This is common across many faiths, where immersion in water or sprinkling with water is used in baptisms and other rites of purification.

We can certainly layer all these meanings onto those given for this rune.

The mundane meaning of Laguz is water and fluidity, perhaps a voyage across water (especially if it appears with Raido or Ehwaz) or some watery event happening in your life – perhaps a hint to lag your pipes! It can speak not only of voyages across water, but of trade and profit. But in deeper terms, this translates to the soul journey, and Laguz may combine with nearby runes to show you areas of concern, where you need to work harder on issues that affect your karmic burden or your relationship with divinity.

Water has a strong relationship with the Moon, which influences tides across the world as well as the emotional rhythms of people, and the Laguz rune aligns with the zodiac sign Cancer. Much folk- and magical lore surrounds water, with holy wells being revered as sacred places (especially in Cornwall, where I live), also sacred rivers and streams. Evil spirits and bad witches cannot cross running water, say the myths, and contaminated things can be cleansed by being left under running water for three or nine days.

The healing and purifying qualities of water are legendary, of course, with wells and springs with healing properties – and other magical qualities – cropping up in all cultures. Norse belief had its share of magical wells, including the three at the roots of Yggdrasil; that of Mimir, which granted inspiration; Hvergelmir, the well in which the dragon Nidhöggr lives and the Well of Wyrd, which, as it watered Yggdrasil, basically supported the entire cosmos (as well as being the place of origin of the runes) – again life-giving.

Water, especially the sea, speaks to us in so many ways and, as a race, the British – and the Norsemen before us – have a lot invested in the sea, we perhaps see more in it than do other races. Our English language is full of often unrecognised nautical expressions.

Water can also be a metaphor and a pathway for voyages of personal discovery, travel along your spiritual path or towards your personal destiny. So Laguz can speak of partings, sacrifices and emotional reactions, of natural forces overwhelming people. And as the ocean often returns things long lost, it also speaks of karma, and of revenge, returns and inheritances. It can speak of cycles, for water moves in an endless cycle, from the clouds to the land, from the land to streams and rivers, so back to the sea to be taken up by the clouds again.

Laguz tells of the unstoppable nature of water, its rhythms that go on forever, and no man can stop them. The strongest dam ever built by man is a hostage to time. Dripping water wears away stone. And at its most merciless, water can overwhelm the strongest swimmer, so Laguz also tells of being overwhelmed by natural forces beyond one's control, whether this is a natural disaster of some kind — though this would probably be the murkstave rather than the upright rune — or a passion from within, like falling madly in love.

So, what's with the sea monster thing? It is a curious fact that, wherever there's a large body of water, you'll find legends of a water monster, from Jenny Greenteeth and the Zennor Mermaid to the Loch Ness Monster and her cousins in regions across the world. Gaze at the surface of any large area of water for any amount of time and you can understand where these stories come from: untamed water calls these ancient beliefs from us in some way that we don't quite understand. Laguz is therefore tied to the Jungian concept of the collective unconscious, which can generate monsters which surface sometimes in our dreams and which can appear as warnings of mental illness or breakdown, or as symptoms of other health crises, or maybe even warnings from the world beyond.

Magically, Laguz can help with healing and purification and, when bound with runes like Raido and Algiz, can protect the traveller.

Murkstave: danger of being overwhelmed, confusion, inner turmoil, the possibility of mental illness.

Leif: It has rained all month and my fields are flooded.
Jayden: Work has just been coming at me all week — I'm overwhelmed.

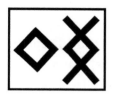

INGWAZ (NG as in 'sing') sex and procreation

PRONOUNCE EENG-waz

ASSOCIATIONS Freyr and Freyja

The original form of this rune may represent a woman's vulva (in a very stylised form, as the runes contain no curved lines) or the head of a penis and yes, it's about sex. Sometimes *Inguz*, this rune changed very early on to the larger form depicted, as the old rune masters clearly felt it should be the same height as the other runes. Some people have commented that the later rune looks like the DNA spiral, which is a very good way of remembering it and understanding what it is all about. Centuries before DNA was discovered, its essence was in this rune.

Because this rune is quite simple in its meaning layers, it will rely more than other runes on the outcome of the runecast — always take note of nearby runes and how they lie in relation to one another. Ingwaz may not be as simple as it seems if it is tied in with stronger runes.

Ingwaz is associated with the ancient God Ing or Ingvi, who later became an aspect of Freyr. Its mundane meaning is sex, passion and fertility. It is the magic that draws together man and woman, or man and man, or woman and woman, that of sexual attraction. It includes good, old-fashioned romance: remember that Freyr sacrificed his magical sword — and thus condemned himself to death at Ragnarök, for love of the beautiful giantess Gerda, who became his wife.

Ingwaz speaks of desire and of orgasm, and then of the creation of new life that may follow. It can also speak of a great surge of energy, of potential stored for some time and then released in some creative process not related to sex.

Ingwaz is concerned more with the body than other runes, and can speak of the importance of keeping your body in good health, eating the right foods and exercising, getting enough sleep and paying attention to personal grooming as well... because you never know! Don't forget that Freud, whether you agree with him or not, thought that almost everything we do is related to sex. So Ingwaz urges you to follow a healthy regime, including healthy recreational sex, and it can also speak of the health of the planet as a whole, and our involvement in this.

Drawing this rune can mean you will meet someone, someone to whom you are strongly attracted and, all being well, the relationship will head in promising directions, including that of the bedroom. That is just one meaning.

If the starting question began with 'Who...?' then this rune may indicate the appearance of a person to whom you are strongly attracted... we're talking full on, mouth open, eyes bulging, virtual lobotomy-style attraction, the kind that can turn you from a well-balanced middle management executive to a stammering moron. Whether that will develop into a Netflix-and-chill scenario may be indicated by nearby runes.

However, its most important meaning is that of blood connections, the inheritance of parents and grandparents and great grandparents before you, all connected by blood and importantly by the act of sex, all very primal scene. It could, in connection with other runes, be telling you that you need to look at your own DNA for the resolution of problems in your life, that you need to dig deep into your own antecedents. Your physical bloodline, your ancestry, is coming to the fore and having its say. This is the rune that might warn of an inherited tendency to high cholesterol or arthritis and bring your parents' and grandparents' lives and the paths they took strongly to your mind. It is 'in the blood', as we say. Meaning; in our genetic make-up, making that DNA spiral shape of this rune very appropriate.

The connection goes on, and the rune may speak of your own contributions to your children's future, what you pass down to them in terms of genetics or of upbringing.

Ingwaz is also a general fertility rune associated with the earth, with plants and crops and livestock, with the mystery found within the magic of a single seed and the miracle of conception. It can have similar meanings to Fehu and Jera in this respect but will probably be about human fertility rather than animal or plant.

The God Ing united the peoples of the North, so his rune can also point to similar scenarios of peace, unity and harmony, probably in a national rather than individual sense.

It can also mean a one-off opportunity coming your way. One that, if it is not accepted, will not be repeated, and although this sounds like an offer of sex, it may or may not be unrelated to romance.

Magically, Ingwaz is an obvious choice for love spells, but also can be used as a container to hold energies ready for release during magical workings or at the right moment. It is also useful as a reinforcement if you are doing sex magic.

Murkstave: this rune is not reversible.

Leif: The new baby has red hair… just like my mother.
Jayden: Getting my DNA tested this week. There's heart disease on my
  dad's side of the family.

DAGGAZ (D) day, cycle, awakening, breakthrough

PRONOUNCE exactly as it looks.
ASSOCIATIONS Baldr, Eostre and Verdandi.

The Sun rises. Cue Grieg's *Morning Song*... you awaken, yawn, stretch, and are ready for the day. This rune is about all the things that this brings to mind: awakenings, enlightenment, new beginnings, breakthroughs... but let's meet the rune properly.

Daggaz is from the same stem as our word 'day'. It has been suggested that its form is based on the lemniscate, the infinity symbol, created without curves. This symbol was known in very ancient times. Or I favour the idea that it illustrates the equinoxes when night equals day. One source suggested seeing this rune as an hourglass on its side, which is a useful way of remembering its shape and meaning.

Daggaz speaks of the day before you and all that it holds, and its ending, a complete cycle. Day after day after day, is how we experience our lives, as Jera speaks of the cycle of a year. So, it speaks of certainty and routine, even security. As Thomas Hardy said, 'Yet this will go onward the same/ Though Dynasties pass.' The Sun will come up tomorrow and things will go on the same. One is reminded of the Norse belief that the very Sun would be killed at the end of all things, eaten by the Fenris wolf, but her daughter would take her place so that life could go on.

As we found, Daggaz is a counterpart to the rune Jera, which speaks of a complete cycle too, a year, and these runes both speak of the quarter days; the solstices and equinoxes. Daggaz and Jera are both runes of change, but change within sameness. Jera signifies the gentle changes of the year and Daggaz the more dramatic changes that a day can bring. But both speak of complete cycles and the march of life, going on and on, round and round again. The rune says, move on, progress, go with the flow. The Old Norse word for Yule, *Jul*, meant a wheel, as in the Wheel of the Year, eternally turning round and round, and the round wheel shape has been associated with the day and the year in many cultures, perhaps because the Sun is round. Daggaz can be likened to the Tarot card Wheel of Fortune, which speaks of the cyclical and inevitable rise and fall of all things. Like Sowelu, it is a positive rune, but has a different range of meanings.

But what else can *day* mean to us? Light, for sure, and enlightenment. Perhaps we have 'slept on' something and we have woken up with the answer. Perhaps this is your day, your day for action, for success. *Carpe diem*, says this rune: seize the day. As the rune is linked to the equinoxes, it also speaks of balance and of liminal states, as the equinoxes are liminal. The Latin word *limen* means a threshold, and Daggaz may well speak of a threshold: of learning, experience or some other aspect of the human condition. Doesn't it look rather like a gate or a pair of swing doors – like those saloon doors in old westerns? Or even, with a small stretch of the imagination, a pair of old-fashioned windows being flung open, as the beautiful heroine of the movie draws a deep breath of the morning air and starts her new day. You stand with your feet on the threshold of something... can the light give you the courage to take that first step? This rune says it can, and that this is the time to do it.

Moving on, Daggaz can talk of attaining spiritual and mystical inspiration, of *seeing the light* in other ways. The dark night of the soul is over, and we have come forth into daylight. The dawn has begun *and all the misbelieving and black horde of fears and sorrows that infest the soul,* the terrors of the night, will fade away with the growing light. And yet they too are part of the cycle, and must have their allotted time. For, without fear, loss, grief, how can there be happiness? Without dark there can be no light — as the two-sided shape of the rune indicates.

Daggaz urges you to see both sides of a question — or both sides of a person. The colleague who snarled at you for nothing may be facing some crisis in his private life; the in-law who apparently hates you may be suffering from some inner turmoil or illness or feels threatened by you in some way. Use your eyes and your perceptions to full capacity, says the rune.

Murkstave: this rune is not reversible.

Leif: The Sun is up, and Frida is lighting the fire, as she does every morning: time to go and milk the cows, check the fences, collect eggs and turn out the pigs to forage. Every day the same but different, praise the Gods!
Jayden: My desktop kit is feeling its age, this is the day I finally sort out my desktop refresh.

OTHILA (O) homeland, homecoming, origins

PRONOUNCE o-THEEL-ah
ASSOCIATIONS Odin

Now we come to the very last rune: the homecoming.

In some runic alphabets Othila (sometimes *Othala*) sits next to Ingwaz. Where Ingwaz is the inheritance of blood, of physical characteristics, of family; Othila is about where you come from, your home.

The meaning of Othila is 'ancestral hall' and it speaks of your roots, the place where you were born or grew up, your ancestry or inheritance. Whether this is a carven timbered palace on the plains, or a tiny hut made up of laths and mud, a five-bedroomed mansion in Chelsea or a council flat in Basingstoke, it is in your bones – literally; as we now know, biologists can tell where someone grew up from the chemical make-up of their skeleton.

This stave is a little more difficult to identify as a shape, but I think that with a little imagination, you can see it as a pictogram of a funny little crooked house with a pointed roof, the kind of twee image you might find on a gift shop sign saying, *Home Sweet Home*.

This rune speaks of your background. Where Ingwaz is about your genetic inheritance, Othila is about your birth circumstances; whether you were born poor or with a silver spoon in your mouth, while other runes nearby may indicate how that will impact on your life. It is more about property than blood. The Norsemen didn't go a-viking for the scenery or their health; they were actually quite materialistic, and their aim was to bring back as much plunder as they could to their families and tribes. They valued wealth and property, and judged men very much by what they owned – pretty much as many people judge others today. But where in our society children from the poorest backgrounds can still achieve a good education and go on to build a success story, the Norsemen were very much bound to the state to which they were born – it defined them pretty much for life – thrall, peasant or nobleman.

Othila speaks of property, and the most obvious meaning of this is a home or property that we have inherited, but it can also speak of other inherited possessions: the things you own – do you have an Old Master in your attic? Do you own a complete library of first editions, or a box of jewellery inherited from Grandma that you have never had valued? Possessions mean a lot to most of us; they give us pleasure, validate our personalities, enhance our homes and maybe even represent unrealised wealth if they are saleable. To those of us who practise magic, they can mean even more: our named athames, our cauldrons, our pentacles and wands are a part of us.

On a mundane level, Othila speaks of home, of homecomings or of acquiring a home through purchase or inheritance. It can speak of feeling at home somewhere you have recently moved to, even in an employment situation – we say 'getting your feet under the table' as an alternative to feeling at home.

Moving on, the homecoming can be a psychological one: the experience of teenagers the world over, who rebel against everything their parents stand for, then find as they grow older that the eternal verities still hold good and perhaps their parents did have something after all. Not just teenagers either; how many times have we heard of lapsed Roman Catholics who, as they enter old age or illness, return to the faith of their childhood for its comfort? Or older people who move 'back home' when their working life is done, in order to be near family or once dear and familiar places.

Spiritually, the rune speaks of that place seekers come to when they have thoroughly explored their path and its possibilities, of contentment, of having come home in a spiritual sense, of reaping the harvest of years of study, work and ritual; in a word, achieving grace. Many of us in paganism and Wicca have had that experience, of finding our true path and feeling that we have finally come home after years of seeking.

Murkstave: where most reversed runes are quite negative, this can carry the meaning that a disregarded piece of property may actually be of great value. And not just property either; it could mean anything you have inherited, including advice. But it can also speak in a more negative way of your ancestral feelings, warning perhaps against xenophobia and prejudice of all kinds.

Leif: I farm this land, and my father before me, and his before him. We are one with the land.

Jayden: Amber's always taking the piss out of me 'cos I come from Sussex, calling me a turnip-muncher. She's such a townie!

Figures in a Runic Landscape

Where Norse culture seemed pretty male-oriented, Norse mythology is no more inclusive; featuring larger-than-life heroes, dreadful battles and the accumulation of treasures. Again, females generally only appear as objects, even Goddesses are subject to abductions and forced marriages rather than having any adventures of their own, and the lower classes of this society hardly feature at all. Yet Norse society was made up of three main levels: thralls, who were in effect slaves; churls, who were free farmers and could own land; and the nobles.

Even the afterlife was arranged around these differences, with men who died in battle going to Odin's glorious hall Valhalla (House of the Slain) or to Freyja's land Folkvangr (Field of the People), and the rest of us being shunted off to several possible destinations such as Hel's hall, Ran's realm under the sea for those who drowned, or even reincarnation into the body of a newborn relative. Or the dead could simply stay and hang out in their own burial mounds (remember the scary episode with the Barrow-wight in *Lord of the Rings*?).

The Norse cosmos was constructed over and around the eternal cosmic tree Yggdrasil, usually identified as an ash tree, a vast structure that delved down into the bottom of the Universe with its roots and with its upper branches touched the sky. All beings lived in the nine worlds held in Yggdrasil's branches, from the giants and the dead to the Gods themselves, and not forgetting Midgard – Tolkien's *Middle Earth* – which is the world we humans know and inhabit.

Almost uniquely among the pantheons of the world, the Norse Gods are distinctly mortal: they can be killed, and their ultimate destruction is foretold; they will almost all perish at Ragnarök, the end of the world, when the forces of darkness rise up and destroy the Sun and the world. They are even reliant on magic apples, kept by a Goddess called Idunn, to keep them young; without these fruits they would age and wither like anyone else.

The Norse Gods are best known to us today through the names they gave our days of the week: Tiw's Day, Woden's (Odin's) Day, Thor's Day and Frigga's or Freyja's Day (Freyja and Frigga tend to have blurred boundaries; no one is quite sure whether or not they are the same Goddess). But to have a really deep understanding of the runes, you are going to have to get to know them better, especially Odin, who gave the runes to Mankind.

The runes, their meanings and history are inextricably bound up with Norse mythology, so it's quite important to have at least a working knowledge of who was who and what they did in Norse belief. Most of the runes are associated with one or more Gods, and to really understand them, you need to understand the nature and the legends of the ruling deity of each, and I would add the relevance of these figures in the 21st century. For they do live on, in stories, in films, in art and music and in the beliefs of modern pagans who still honour them.

Odin

Let's start with the CEO. Odin, or Oðinn, is the King of the Gods and the ruler of Asgard, home of the Aesir, or main Norse Gods (just to complicate things, there are two sets of Gods living in different worlds, but also mingling. Aesir, BTW, is pronounced ass-EER). In Germany and Saxony, he was known as Woden.

I expect you are all thinking of a version of Jupiter or Zeus, perhaps with a couple of horns tacked onto his headgear to show he's Norse. Wrong. Odin (I'll go with the spelling we 21st century Anglo Saxons and other English speakers feel happier with) is not at all a typical pantheon head. Where the classical rulers of the Gods seemed to leave their celestial thrones only for a bit of extracurricular skirt-chasing, Odin is an adventurer, a warrior, an explorer, a psychopomp, a shaman… a scientist. In terms of the Gods of other cultures, he aligns with Mercury, Hermes, Thoth, Taliesin and Ogma as a God of secret wisdom and knowledge, and of communication, and nowadays IT – what, you thought a Norse deity would be unable to get his head around modern technology? (Incidentally, I'm *not* going to mention the runic Bluetooth logo at this point, as it's been done to death!)

Odin discovered the runes by putting himself through a terrible ordeal, hanging upside down over the Well of Wyrd for nine days without food or drink, and wounding his own side with a spear (that one rings some bells).

You might have an image of him as some horned helmet-wearing biker dude clashing his mead cup against his sword and throwing bones to the wolfhounds in his ancient hall, maybe overlaid with images of the actor Anthony Hopkins. Probably a better way of thinking of him is as a sort of Gandalf with overtones of Santa (very good reasons for both of these). There is so much more to him than you could anticipate. Yes, he certainly has his biker dude side (he is said to lead the Wild Hunt), and many other sides as well. He also has an abundance of names. The Norsemen were fond of *kennings*, simple riddles based on their legends and stories, which were used to give alternative names to people, Gods and items as a way to demonstrate the speaker's wit and knowledge. The sea, for example, might be called 'the fishes' bath', and a ship a 'sea-horse'. Odin has plenty of names based on kennings, and also on descriptions of him and his attributes, such as *Gangleri*: 'Wanderer', or *Runatyr*: God of Runes, or *Galdrafödr*: father of magical chants.

All the runes belong to Odin, of course, but one or two are especially close to his heart: Ansuz, the rune of the breath of life and communication (Mercury again!), Othila, the rune of home, and Ehwaz, that of work and partnership.

Odin does not walk alone: with him are his familiars, as befits an über-shaman. The closest to him are the ravens that perch on his shoulders.

- **Huginn and Muninn** (Thought and Memory). Ravens have long been sacred birds in countries to which they are native, and these wise creatures (Corvids are among the most intelligent of birds) fly hither and yon, bringing Odin news and knowledge from all the nine worlds.

- **Geri and Freki** (Hungry and Greedy). At his heels run his wolves, just like a pair of dogs. Unlike the ravens, they do not seem to have a specific function, but wolves are deeply associated with Odin, who feeds these two from his own plate, consuming only wine himself.

- **Sleipnir.** Sleipnir is a rather difficult to imagine horse who has eight legs and is therefore magically able to travel anywhere faster than any other creature, even to carry his rider Odin through the sky... and if you're thinking of reindeer and sacks of presents, you're not wrong. Odin was said to fly through the sky on Sleipnir at Yule, bringing gifts for his people, which is clearly the origin of some of our Christmas imagery.

    Sleipnir was born to the God Loki as a result of an adventure involving his shapeshifting into a mare to lure away an enemy's stallion, on one of the occasions he was acting on the side of the Gods. Loki disappeared from Asgard for a while, then returned with a magnificent horse with eight legs, which he presented to Odin – apparently quite without embarrassment.

Sleipnir's image was used by shamans and magicians as a charm to protect travellers and horses. I have used him myself in an amulet to protect horses in a stable where the tragic death of a horse had apparently left some kind of residual behind which was distressing them. And in fact, the symbol for horse, the rune Ehwaz, was used widely in amulets, and seemed to have a magical meaning by itself for the Norsemen. To them it was a totemic animal, and was frequently sacrificed to the Gods, as something valuable enough to make a fitting offering. To ancient peoples like the Norsemen, the horse was the very basis for their success, both in battle and agriculture.

- **Mimir's head.** Odin is often pictured with the head of the God Mimir tucked under his arm. Mimir was esteemed as the wisest of the Aesir, to whom Odin himself lost an eye as the price of drinking from his well of inspiration. At the end of the war between the two races of Gods, Mimir was one of two of the Aesir sent to Vanaheim, while Kvasir, Njörd, Freyr and Freyja were brought to Asgard. Sadly, the Vanir murdered him and, when Odin learned of this, he collected his friend's head, embalmed it with herbs and kept it with him. The head continues to talk to Odin and advise him wisely.

- **Valkyries.** These female demigods hovered over the battlefield, carrying away Odin's share of the valiant slain to his hall Valhalla. The meaning of 'val' in Valkyrie and Valhalla does not come from the same root as our word 'valiant', it means 'killed' or 'slain', but it is a useful way of remembering the ideas and images behind these words.

Thor

Every female reader's thoughts will turn to the portrayal of the Thunder God by Chris Hemsworth in the Marvel franchise films.

Nope, that's just not right. This actor is just way too.... *pretty* to be Thor. Thor is a total badass, a giant-like figure, brandishing his terrible war-hammer Mjöllnir, with which he is perfectly ready to beat in the head of anyone who crosses him or happens to be a giant. He doesn't waste time with niceties; he acts, and usually violently. It's easy to see Thor as a monosyllabic (and perhaps not very bright) violent ruffian; but he is also the protector of Gods and men alike, and especially of the poorer classes, the thralls and the peasant farmers, who pass into his safekeeping at death. And his hammer was obviously seen by the Norse as a symbol of fertility and blessing, as its facsimiles were used in rituals of birth and the dead.

Frigg or Frigga

This majestic lady is Odin's wife and queen, and in some ways relates to Hera/Juno in classical mythology. Yet she is rather a shadowy figure who may be just another aspect of Freyja – they do seem to share Odin. Her areas of influence are the home, family, hospitality and motherhood.

Freyr and Freyja

These two, being twins, often come as BOGOFs, though they have very distinct personalities as individuals. They are members of the Vanir Gods, as opposed to the Aesir. Where the Aesir are mainly Gods of glory and battle, the Vanir are Gods of magic, nature, and fertility who dwell in their own realm of Vanaheim. You can think of them as being like Tolkien's elves; beautiful, elusive forest-dwellers who care for nature. Freyr and Freyja live in the Aesir city of Asgard, though, as sort of hostages or consuls after the war between the two races of Gods was resolved.

I mentioned Chris Hemsworth as Thor in the Marvel films. Put him in a green cloak instead of a red, take away the outsized hammer and you would have the perfect Freyr: basically, sex on a stick. Freyr's domain is fertility: crops, livestock and human love.

He is such a romantic that he gives up his magical sword for the sake of the woman (or in this case, giantess) he loves, thus condemning himself to a gory death at Ragnarök, the final battle of the Gods.

His sister Freyja is a sort of Norse Aphrodite with golden hair, and it's easy to see her just as that, and not take her too seriously. But she is so much more: she shares with the Greek Hecate and Egyptian Isis the patronage of magic and witches, and when Odin is gathering the souls of those slain in battle, she takes a half-share of the harvest. She is a powerful figure who is quite capable of standing up to Odin himself. Alone, of the Norse Goddesses she appears as a vivid personality and has her own adventures, including going off to have a gangbang with four dwarf goldsmiths in order to get her dream necklace Brisingamen made for her. The necklace has a name, as almost all artefacts in Norse mythology, and in Norse everyday life, seem to have, yet there does not seem to be any indication that it was a magical necklace.

This Goddess was said to weep tears of gold, and amongst her attributes was a feathered cloak which enabled her to fly, and a chariot drawn by cats (very appropriate for an über-witch).

As these Gods' names are spelled in the original Norse, it is hard to see how to differentiate them when speaking. Freyja is easier: her name is said, FRAY-yah, whilst her brother's name is pronounced more like FREER. The terminal R of his name (which is often Anglicised to Frey) was a normal masculine ending.

Loki

Loki is an intriguing character, and it is hard to psychoanalyse him. Why is he such a bastard? He often seems to be on a self-destruct course, doing everything he can to provoke the other Gods into losing their cool and murdering him. But at other times, he is clearly a team player, full of ideas to help them win against the giants and other foes. There is a poem called The Flyting of Loki in which he arrives at a gathering of the Gods and goes from one to another, insulting each one to his or her face and giving a good impression of someone hoping to be set on and killed. His obnoxious banter even includes mocking the Queen of Asgard, Frigga, to her face about the death of her beloved son Baldr – for which Loki himself is responsible. When Thor arrives, Loki baits him as well... and even gets away with that. The explanation is that he is a God of Fire, Storm and Chaos. He isn't a Norse equivalent of the Devil, though he does do some pretty nasty things, including causing Baldr's death by trickery. But it *is* this 'roast' of the Gods that finally gets him put away; they bind him and imprison him in a cave with a poisonous snake dripping venom on to his face... and there he will stay until Ragnarök.

The Children of Loki

- **Hel.** I always felt Hel had a bit of a bum deal. In Norse belief, the Trickster God Loki had three monstrous children with a giantess, the wolf Fenrir (or Fenris-wolf), Jörmungandr, later the Midgard Serpent, and a daughter who was half beautiful maiden and half rotting corpse. This girl was sent down to rule over the inglorious dead, i.e. those who had not died in battle; and became the Goddess of the Underworld. She is not on the side of the angels, though I hesitate to use those overworked words, good and evil, when speaking of any pagan Gods. It is useful to understand her nature in looking at her own rune Hagalaz: what would you expect from a Queen of Hell who has seen her father chained and poisoned and her brothers and half-brothers similarly taken from her, and though she herself has done no harm, she has been hurled down Yggdrasil to rule over the dead in the cold and dark. At Ragnarök, she will hurtle through the gates of Hel at the head of the armies of the dead and darkness to join her father and brothers in the battle.

- **Fenrir/Fenris Wolf.** Fenrir grows into a big strong boy, so big and strong that the Gods become very uneasy, and decide this dog needs a collar. See the section below on **Tyr** for the full account of Fenrir's chaining. The chain does not prevent him from fathering two sons, who remain free to do mischief. Hati and Sköll are two wolves that pursue, respectively, the Moon and the Sun through the sky, hoping to eat them. At Ragnarök they will succeed, plunging the world into darkness. Norse mythology is full of supernatural wolves.

Fenrir frees himself from his magical chains at Ragnarök, and distinguishes himself by eating Odin, but pays for this action with his life, slain by Odin's son Vidarr, who tears him in half.

- **Jörmungandr, the Midgard Serpent.** The third child is a snake, which Thor picks up and tosses into the sea, but once there Jörmungandr grows to a monstrous size until he is able to encircle the whole of Midgard (which is seen as a disc, not a sphere) and bite his own tail. In one story, Thor goes fishing with a giant ox-head for bait, and hooks Jörmungandr by accident.

  At the end of the world, the snake is the one who kicks off Ragnarök by letting go of his tail, and thereafter he rises from the boiling seas to take part in the battle, biting Thor fatally with his poisonous fangs. Thor kills the serpent, but then falls, dying from the poisonous bite.

Tyr

To give you a little context for this God and his rune Teiwaz; as I mentioned, the Gods had to decide what to do with Loki's children by a giantess. These children were brought to Asgard while the Gods debated what to do about them, though they had already decided that their blood could not be spilled on the sacred ground of the Gods' home. Thor solved part of the problem by tossing the snake into the ocean, and the girl, Hel, was sent down to become Goddess of the Dead. The Gods agreed that the wolf would have to be bound, so they popped off to Fetters R Us and came back with two huge chains, which they tried on him, one after the other. He broke them both without even trying. A magical chain was then procured, made from such strange ingredients as the beards of women, the teeth of birds, the roots of stones and the sound of a cat walking. When Fenrir saw this slender chain, he smelled a giant Norse rat, and refused to be bound with it unless one of the Gods put his hand in his jaws as a kind of hostage. Only Tyr was brave enough to do this – and when the wolf could not break the chain, Tyr lost his hand as a result, earning the epithet 'Bravest of the Gods'. His loss was a sign of utter courage, but also the price he paid for deceiving and breaking his word to the wolf. He played an important role in oath-taking for the Norse and was seen as the epitome of justice and honour.

Heimdallr

The Gods' city Asgard is reached by a magical bridge, the rainbow Bifrost, and anyone trying to cross this must get past Heimdallr, chief of security for the Aesir, who spends his life in watchfulness and has a magical horn called Gjallarhorn which can be heard in all the worlds when it is blown. Some Norse legends have him fathering mankind as well (busy guy!), so he is more personally concerned with ordinary people than some of the other Gods.

The Norns

These are very intriguing figures who have a lot in common with the Fates, or Moirai, of classical mythology. They can be regarded as the original owners of the runes, as they tend the Well of Wyrd, from whence Odin drew them. They are three giantesses or Goddesses (remember, the line between God and giant can be quite blurry in Norse belief), sisters called Urd (or Wyrd), the past; Verdandi (pronounced vair-DANDY), the present; and Skuld (Skoold), the future, and they dwell at the roots of Yggdrasil, the cosmic tree, watering its roots with water drawn from the well. There were also a great many lesser norns, with a small N, who would show up at a birth with gifts – not always good ones – for the child, determining its fate as it grew.

Wyrd and Orlog

The Norsemen had a fair amount of understanding of the human psyche, and a rich system of myth and story to help with understanding this, which is why Norse mythology is so important in understanding the runes. Like modern pagans, they saw all people and objects as connected, and the word they used to describe this connectedness was 'Wyrd', which hovers in meaning somewhere between fate and magic. Though it is clearly the ancestor of our word 'weird' it did not originally mean weird in the sense of odd or eerie but referred to the cosmic web that influences and is influenced by all beings and events – like 'The Force' in the Star Wars films. The three Norns were in charge of this web and, if your belief system permits, it is probably a good idea to also ask them for their blessing as you use the runes.

Wyrd is a concept similar to the Greek idea of fate, which was also administrated by three Goddesses. However, it seems to have been less personal than the classical idea; a web of events going on throughout the world, in which humans and Gods alike might become entangled, and could also influence by their own actions. Wyrd could also be affected by magic, as everything was connected – a bit like broadband, which can allow malware and viruses to access your set-up if you aren't careful.

Orlog, which aligns closely with the Eastern concept of karma and dharma, was about the far-reaching effects of actions and consequences and carried on the idea of personal actions influencing one's fate. The Norse did not see people as helpless in the face of destiny, but as beings that forged their own destinies by their actions.

Audhumla

She is the cosmic cow who created life, licking away the frost with her warm tongue, thawing the Gods who were concealed under the ice, and defrosting the world so things could grow.

Baldr

This intriguingly Christ-like figure is the son of Odin and Frigga and a resplendent deity adored by all for his beauty, wisdom and goodness. All, that is, except Loki, whose spite and jealousy bring about Baldr's death and that of his poor blind brother Hödur, Loki's patsy. Appropriately for a sun God, Baldr is slain by a twig of mistletoe — perhaps an echo of ancient royal human sacrifice — and the Norse legends give a grim description of something that sounds like a nuclear winter as a result. But after Ragnarök, Baldr — and Hödur — are released from Hel, and he then returns to rule over the regenerated cosmos, one of the few male Gods to survive into the next age.

Eostre

This is the name of a Germanic Goddess of the Spring, with a thing for hares. She gives us our word Easter and the Easter Bunny, and the neopagan Sabbat of Ostara at the vernal equinox is associated with her. She is a Goddess of new beginnings and of the revival of the earth after winter.

Njörd

The Norse Sea God is a member of the Vanir who relocated to Asgard after the war between the two races of Gods. He is the father of Freyr and Freyja by an unknown Goddess, said to be his sister, possibly the Earth Goddess Nerthus. He also had a giantess wife called Skadi, but the marriage did not last. The cult of this God continued into the 18th and 19th centuries, with fishermen thanking him for a good catch.

Nerthus

This Earth Goddess is a lesser-known deity, whose mysteries centred on a cart which only her priests were allowed to touch. Her festival included the cart, drawn by heifers, going on a procession around the countryside to bless the people (a common religious custom in Norse culture), before the image of the Goddess was washed in a sacred lake by slaves who were afterwards drowned, as nobody who had seen this sacred mystery could live to tell the tale. Because her name seems to have some etymological relationship to that of Njörd, she may be his sister-wife and mother of Freyr and Freyja. It is frustrating how much of Norse belief has been lost over the ages.

Skadi

This frost giantess, a patroness of skiing and hunting, is the daughter of Thiazi, a giant killed by the Gods for abducting Idunn, the Goddess who keeps the magical apples that keep the Gods young. As compensation for her loss, she is allowed to choose one of the Gods as a husband – but can only choose him by his bare feet. Skadi is hoping for the beautiful and gentle Baldr and chooses two good-looking feet she thinks must be his, so is a little put out when she finds she has chosen Njörd, and the marriage is short lived. According to one poem, she later marries Odin.

Sunna

Oddly to our eyes, the Norsemen saw the Sun as female, as a beautiful and golden Goddess who drove her magnificent chariot, drawn by two magical horses, across the sky every day. Her blessings must have been especially appreciated by these dwellers in cold and often dark regions, where the polar night occurs every midwinter. Fortunately, she has a beautiful daughter, for she is destined to die at Ragnarök, eaten by Fenrir or his son Sköll. But her daughter takes her place in the new world that is to come.

Surtr

This is one of the major bad guys, a fire giant who rises up at Ragnarök to fight against the Gods, and kills Freyr (who, you remember, lost his magical sword as the price for marrying Gerda, the beautiful giantess).

Völund

Known in English as Wayland, this legendary elven blacksmith and artisan is mentioned in many stories, including the Elder Edda, in which his tale is told in The Lay of Völund. Taken prisoner and robbed of his treasures by a villainous king as he waits alone for his lover, Völund is deliberately crippled and forced to work, creating jewellery and other wonders for his captor. Using his cunning arts, he takes a terrible revenge on the king and his family, killing his sons and making drinking cups from their skulls, and raping his daughter.

Ymir

This primordial giant emerged from the ice at the beginning of time and created beings from his own body. The Gods killed him and fashioned the cosmos from his body, using his bones as rocks and mountains, his flesh as earth, his skull as the vault of the sky, his hair and beard as plants, his brains as the clouds and his blood as the seas and rivers.

CHAPTER FOUR

Getting Kitted Out

There are plenty of books and websites out there that will teach you all the nuances of each and every stave and recite the ancient rune poems from which we derive what knowledge we have of them. You can learn all about what the Teiwaz rune means, or why Berkana is considered a feminine rune or what Ingwaz, the sex rune, might have to say about your family. But once you have assimilated this knowledge you are bound to be hungry for more, to take the study of the runes to its next logical step: to use them for magic and spiritual practice. As the 21st century goes on, more and more people are taking an interest in the ancient wisdoms, in Wicca and witchcraft, in Asatru/Heathenry, in Druidry, and in magic and divination. This may be a reaction to the society in which we find ourselves; in which a child can have three biological parents and workers can be microchipped into their office IT set-ups: many people feel a need to return to Nature and traditional 'analog' ways of living. But now is now, we can't change it, and there really is no need to go and live off the grid in a shack made of branches in the woods, to live an exciting, meaningful and magical life.

If you are drawn to the runes, it is for a reason, and you should certainly explore this fascinating system. Acquiring a set of your own is the first step. You can find gorgeous sets in magic shops and online; made from crystals, wood, ceramics and glass; I've even found rune dice on websites. But... you know what I'm going to say, don't you? If you really want to take your study of the runes seriously, you should: hashtag #MakeYourOwnSet, always, always, though this will involve some pain!

The Norsemen would have used pieces of wood, as the most readily available medium, and this would be my first choice as well. If possible, use wood from a tree that is considered sacred, or is special to you. The Norsemen revered the ash above all, but there are other trees that have magical associations, such as rowan, elder (not terribly suitable, as its branches tend to be reed-like, with a pithy centre), oak and willow; any tree that is indigenous to your country or that speaks to you personally is okay. Cut the wood according to the pagan principals, asking the tree's permission and leaving it a gift in exchange – a lock of your hair or a silver coin is traditional, but I can't imagine the tree wouldn't prefer a jugful of water with plant food in it. You will need a nice straight branch, 3–4cms in diameter, with at least 30cms of good straight wood. The hard part is cutting the discs, and a table saw is excellent for this, if you have one, or have a kindly neighbour who will let you use his. You will need 24 identical pieces (plus maybe a couple of extras in case you spoil one or lose one).

You can also find wooden discs or square or rectangular wooden tiles, ready cut for crafts, online, but be careful to order the right size: it's all too easy to end up with things the size of saucers. You will need discs (or tiles) that are 3–4cms in diameter and between 0.5 and 1cm thick, 24 all the same size, with a couple of spares, as before. Many of these sites will actually tell you what kind of wood it is, and some sellers can be contacted and asked for custom items.

The wood you have cut yourself, and often the bought discs, come with bark on, and you must decide whether to strip this off or not. Personally, I think the discs look great as nature intended, but do give them a light sanding, not forgetting that every bit of personal contact you have with them ties them closer to you and thus renders them more and more effective as a magical tool.

At this stage, I would magically cleanse and even consecrate the blank wooden pieces, using any ritual you feel comfortable with. I would keep them close to you for a while, perhaps sleep with them under the pillow or on the nightstand, to absorb your personal energies. These dudes are going to be important to you, so it is good to take your time and put every effort into creating them.

Okay, now for the fun bit, the artwork. When I made my own set, I took my time over this, carrying a blank rune about with me until it told me which one it was. I wore it in a cute little decorated suede pouch around my neck (letting curious muggles think it was just an accessory), but your pocket would do just as well (take care it does not end up in the washing machine!). Once I knew which rune it was, I pencilled it on the surface and, when I was happy with the shape, I painted it. Depending on the wood, you may find you need to give the disc a very light coat of clear acrylic first, as some wood may absorb the paint, resulting in a fluffy line instead of the clear hard line you want.

The rune shapes are made up exclusively of straight lines – they were designed for carving easily into wood and stone – and there should not be any curves in your finished designs. This of course makes them much easier to create.

Don't forget to clean up afterwards, rubbing off any pencil marks that show around your rune outline, and obviously if you find you need to give them a primer coat of varnish, make sure the pencilling is done on top of this, or the marks will be there to stay.

I think I mentioned pain. The traditional colour for painting the runes is red, because the Old Norse runemasters would have used their own blood for the artwork, to tie the runes to themselves magically and make them more effective. That's slightly ick, and we don't really want to be hacking at ourselves until we have produced enough claret to paint a whole set of runes, but there is a middle path. A pricked finger will produce one drop, enough to mix in with red acrylic paint, which is then used to paint the rune symbol. And of course, you younger ladies have a much easier source available to you every month. Blood is used a lot by pagans to personalise and consecrate magical items, and when you consider that modern forensic methods can identify and even type old bloodstains — sometimes even after they have been scrubbed up — you will see there is more to this than superstition. It is certainly something I do; in our house you know when I've cut myself whilst chopping food in the kitchen because I'm dashing about looking, not for sticky plasters, but for my latest magical artefact so I can bleed on it!

If you are into pokerwork, this is also a good way to create the symbols and can look pretty fabulous. You don't need an expensive pokerwork tool for this; nick your dad's or partner's soldering iron if you don't have one of your own, but just take lots of care. The iron gets hot enough to cause a serious injury, and very nasty damage can also be caused to polished surfaces if you lay it down carelessly, which could make you unpopular. You can get really creative, dig holes in the discs and embed tiny crystal beads, or inlay the symbols with coloured resins. This is not in the best tradition of the runes, but hey, it's your set.

You can also further personalise your set by putting your own identifying symbol on to the back surface of each rune, whether this is a bindrune, a sigil of some kind or even your own initials. Do make sure they all look the same: it should not be possible to identify any rune unless it is face up.

Once the runes are all created, you can give them a coat of varnish; recommended, as you don't want the paint or any other decoration to wear off as they tumble together in their bag, and then leave them to dry thoroughly. My preference for this is to leave them on a windowsill through at least one lunation, so they get a dose of full moonlight.

If you find the runes stick together because of the varnish, which can happen long after it has dried, put them in a plastic bag and shake in a bit of talcum powder, toss them together – like chicken pieces in seasoned flour – and then tip them out again, knocking off the powder, and you will find that this solves the problem.

Many people will now consecrate their runes, blessing them by the four elements (by passing through incense smoke for air, a candle flame for fire, sprinkling water on them and finally laying them on the ground or on the altar pentacle, a witch's tool that represents the earth. They can also be anointed with magical potions. My choice would be one made from the Nine Sacred Herbs of Odin: betony, crab apple, fennel, lambs' cress, mayweed, mugwort, nettle (stinging), plantain and thyme. All of these are quite common; when I went looking, I found about five of them on my driveway!

I knew someone once who used to create sets of runes from cow bones he bought at the butcher's, cleaning the bones thoroughly by boiling them with laundry powder until they were white and clean. Next, he would carefully saw the bones into long strips, sanding off the natural structures on the interior surfaces, and then saw these lengths across to make little tiles. He created the symbols by gouging them into the surface of the bone with a sharp knife or bradawl, then rubbing in bootblacking to make them stand out – you can get red shoe restorer, which would look more traditional, and of course you could add your drop of blood to it before rubbing it in. These would certainly be stunning, but perhaps not a medium that would sit well with vegetarian or vegan rune students.

Okay, what else will you need?

Your runes are sacred. It is not considered good form to chuck them on the dirty floor to do a reading, or indeed to treat them casually or disrespectfully in any way. Many rune readers use a clean white cloth, even on the table, to make sure their runes do not get dirty or scratched. This can be as simple as you wish, or you can embellish it with symbols or decoration. I have a gorgeous runecasting cloth made for me by a talented friend, which is divided into areas – but we will talk about this later.

If you really are clever, like my friend, you might be able to make yourself a casting cloth that folds up into a bag for your runes, for they will need a storage pouch of some kind to carry them around in. This should be big enough for you to get your hand in and mix the runes about prior to drawing one.

Many pagans also carry a dowsing pendulum, and this is certainly a useful adjunct to the runes. It is also a useful tool for setting up parameters when you are starting out. Again, we will talk about this later.

Do you create a second set of runes just for use in magic? It does save you from having an incomplete set some of the time while some of the staves are gracing your altar or working space as part of a magical set-up that you haven't finished with yet. But this is very much up to you; it's a lot of work to do over again, and there is a case for saying that your own original set will be more powerful because it is your primary set. Unless you plan on taking your runes out to do magic under the Moon in wild places – with the danger of losing some – I would not go to this trouble. Some Tarot packs are available in a much larger format, so you can use these large cards as part of magical workings, and it would perhaps be a good idea to obtain some larger wooden discs – say two or three times the size of your originals – on which to create rune symbols and bindrunes as you require them. If you paint or varnish the discs well, so they are glossy, they can be used over and over, and the symbols just washed or wiped off when they are finished with. For myself, I prefer to use a rune board. This is a plank of wood; mine is 8ins by 12ins, a useful size, which is used just like a blackboard. It is better to stain the wood a darker colour, if it is a light wood, and then give it a light coat of clear acrylic just to seal it – but be careful not to make it shiny, or the chalk will not mark it. You can buy purpose-made blackboard paint too, or matt black emulsion. Runic magic can be created on this board with chalk (I consecrated both the board and the chalk before I used them for the first time), then wiped away when you are done with the spell and it has hopefully worked. Again, you can embellish the board around the sides and corners with sigils or curlicues. Whatever makes it special and magical for you. The board can be used in conjunction with herbs and crystals and, if you make it large enough, it can form a magical altar that can hold everything you need for spellcasting, and double up as a base for crystal grids and other magical work.

The 'props' that you use for magic – and that's just what they are because the power comes from you – are important because they get you in the mood: they are magical foreplay, if you like. That is why you have a sacred space in your home for magic, a consecrated athame, candles, images of the Ancient Ones, incense and so on. It is why you work at night, preferably under the light of the Full Moon.

What other artefacts do you need to practise rune magic? Magic starts with you, and equipment is not really necessary: we're not playing RuneScape® after all. However, as you progress with your skills, you may feel the need to own at least one or two runic tools. The Old Norse runemasters, in addition to the leather pouch of runes carried on their belt, would no doubt have carried a runic staff and perhaps a wand. It is easy to suspect these things were more in the nature of regalia than actual magical tools, like the old shepherds who carried their crooks to the hiring fair to advertise their line of work. They would no doubt have been dressed to the nines to inspire awe and confidence in their abilities. Have a look at this description of a völva (Norse witch) called Thorbjörg, who seems to have been a real historical person:

She was dressed in such a wise: she had a blue mantle over her, with strings at the neck, and inlaid with gems right down the skirt. She wore glass beads around her neck. On her head she had a hood of black lambskin, lined with white catskin. She had a staff in her hand with a knob on the end, ornamented with brass and with gems about the knob. About her she had a girdle of fur, and a large leather bag in which she kept the amulets necessary for her work. She had furry calfskin boots on her feet, tied with long, stout thongs with brass tags at the ends. On her hands she wore gloves of white catskin, furry within.

Dressed to kill, and note the staff, in this case a magical distaff (a length of wood used for winding on unspun fibres ready for spinning, and a symbol in many cultures of the female members of a household) called a seidstafr, which was so important to her that it would have been buried with the völva when she died. The distaff wand possibly symbolised the 'weaving' inherent in Wyrd and the practice of magic. Magic was very much the preserve of the female witch, and indeed brought dishonour to men who practised it, although this does not seem to have stopped them. There is a tale of one king who was so horrified at hearing that his son practised sorcery that he ghosted him – literally, not electronically. He had him murdered, by his own brother. This is hard to understand today, but the Norsemen were macho to the max, and magic seemed to them to be stealthy and underhand, okay for the ladies, but defo not us chaps, you know.

A runic staff may be made very easily, in fact the hardest part, especially if you live in a town, may be acquiring the length of wood. My own feeling is that this should be ash, to resonate with Yggdrasil the World Tree, but for heaven's sake do not go chopping down living trees and despoiling woodland. Ash trees are quite common, blight notwithstanding, and can be found growing in most rural hedgerows. It is a distinctive wood with smooth grey bark and usually completely straight branches. In early spring it has coal-black triangular buds.

At the end of summer, country hedges are often trimmed by machinery, and it may be possible to grab an ash pole then. You need a length a little less than your own height, and sturdy enough for a walking stick.

In some magical traditions a stang is used, and this can certainly become part of your runic practice. It is similar to the staff but is not generally carried; rather it is thrust into the ground at rituals and used as a focus for the work or worship. The stang generally has a forked top, on which items can be hung. However, with both these items, you may feel that they are not as desirable if you happen to live in an urban area, with little chance of joining in pagan outdoor events out in the countryside.

The wand will be easier to acquire, as you only need a length equal to the distance between your elbow and the tip of your forefinger. Again, ash is good for this for the same reasons, and because it is such a straight growing wood.

How you adorn these items is very much up to your own taste, but if they are to be used for rune magic, runic carvings should certainly form part of their embellishment. You could carve your own name, or magical name, into the item or hang discs or tags carved with runes from it, and you could further embellish it with crystals, feathers and charms. These items can look very impressive and 'tribal' when decorated in this fashion.

Other items for your altar can also be personalised with runic carvings. The Norsemen were fond of carving ribbons of runes around the perimeter of pictures carved in wood and stone and remember: the runes can be read from left to right or from right to left. Your pentacle can certainly be carved with runes, either the set of 24 around the circumference, or runic inscriptions saying it belongs to you. Beautiful altar plates or hanging decorations can be created on log slices or pieces cut from planks, with the runes around the edge and a larger symbol, perhaps Aegishjalmur or the knot of Odin in the centre. These items serve both as embellishment for your altar and for the charging of items for spell work or consecration.

Where to keep your runes and tools? My preferred choice for the runes would always be by your bed. They can then absorb your personal energies all night long, and the staves are there on the bedside table ready for you when you want to draw your daily rune. Any other tools are best kept hidden from sight, as you do not want curious friends picking them up and handling them. In the wardrobe behind your clothes for larger items is a place that works for many people. Who goes into your closet?

Last, but not least: a place to work. You may already have a full permanent magical set-up with an altar, deity images, candles and tools, or you may be trying to start your magical practice in a corner of your bedroom: either can work. Be aware of the compass points, as these are important in much magical work and ritual. Find out where north is, and set your working surface, altar or board, against it so you are facing in this direction when you work. For most practitioners in the Northern and Western traditions, north has a special meaning, largely because of the pole and the group of circumpolar stars known as Caer Arianrhod, which are seen to hardly move in the sky compared with the more southerly constellations, and which do not set.

Your magical space is important and privacy is vital to its effectiveness. Unless you are a powerful and experienced witch, you can't do magic in the toilet roll aisle in Asda, or with a houseful of screaming kids and a sink full of dirty dishes. It's like trying to make love in the street with other people all around. Just as with romance, you need the moonlight, a few candles, perhaps some mysterious music: anything that gets you in the mood and gets your magic on. I once joked in a PowerPoint presentation to my local moot that a graveyard might be the best place for spellworking – well, I wasn't totally joking!

If you share your home with others and do not wish them to know about your beliefs, your altar or board can be covered with a clean cloth when not in use, which also allows you to decorate it with magical symbols which are then concealed by the cloth. Have a safe place to keep your magical items, where they can't be picked up and handled by others, perhaps a drawer, or you might even invest in a lockable box big enough to hold all your tools but small enough to slide under the bed. If you have the kind of flatmates who will come bursting in and disrespectfully put their coffee mug or even their feet up on your altar, you can even create a wooden false top for the altar, which is lifted away when you want to work.

If you like to work outdoors, this is great, but make sure the compass app on your phone is on so you can ascertain which direction is north, and again ensure that you are sitting correctly. It's not 100 per cent vital, but it's an observance that will, like so many others, add bang to your runic buck.

It is useful to keep a record or journal of your magical workings and your spiritual progress as well, and this is much easier to keep electronically than in a physical book. It may not look as inspiring as some of these artistic leather journals you can buy, bound with antique-finish brass, tied closed with thongs and with eldritch images etched into the cover, but it is a lot more practical, and easier to keep safe from prying eyes – and don't forget that on a magical path you never stop learning, so perhaps a hard-copy written book isn't the best idea anyway.

I personally spoiled so many beautiful books by making mistakes and then realising things had to be added onto pages where there was no more space, that I gave up in the end and now keep my *Book of Shadows* on the computer, where it can be updated and changed as often as I like. It now occupies some 2.5Gb, as I can store anything, including video, on there. Anything sensitive can be password protected, and do not, of course, forget to back it all up regularly!

The exception to this is a record of your daily rune readings, which is easily kept in a small notebook kept in the bedside drawer, where it can be used when you are first up in the morning, and at night, for 'feedback'. This is a vital habit to get into, at least in the early days of your runic practice: draw one rune every morning — before you have coffee, before you brush your teeth — and record which one it is in your book. Then, at the end of the day, review the events of the day and relate them to the rune. You will be surprised at what this will teach you, and at the often very personal messages the runes will give you. Sometimes, it can seem to a rune reader that they have developed a private language with the staves that another rune reader wouldn't understand. Because, we are all different. Write the book in code or hide it if you have nosy roommates. I can write in Pitman's shorthand, which has proved a boon when it comes to keeping private records.

And now we are ready to get started.

CHAPTER FIVE

Surfing the Web

Does anyone even do that anymore, LOL? But I'm talking about the Web of Wyrd, which actually has quite a lot in common in many ways with the Internet... you are connected to everyone and everything and can interact with them, you meet friends, bloggers, trolls and influencers. It's all quite like an adventure from Norse mythology. And the runes are your pocket guide to this journey, your personal Tripadvisor for each step of the way.

Developing a relationship with your runes starts with creating them but continues with *respecting* them. Draw a rune every day to see what the day will bring. If you don't like the look of the one you have drawn, tough. *Do not draw another one*; this is disrespectful and daft – is your day going to change because you played spoilt kid? What you can do, if you are baffled by the one you have drawn, is ask for clarification and draw one further rune to help you understand what the first one is about (or if not, it could be that the runes are trying to tell you about a situation you didn't even ask about). You may still be puzzled, but the day will bring its own clarification. And developing this habit will teach you the lore of the runes, as each one drawn will give its own lesson as you ponder it. The runes will personalise themselves to you, and you will learn additional meanings for each stave that are meaningful to you alone and are not part of some official canon of given meanings. The runes know, because you know, at some very high level of your being, what is going down, which is not really magical at all: just a method for prodding your right brain awake. But always, the most important part of the work is to lay yourself open to the runes, to ask them in courtesy to grant you some hints of this information. As you get to know your runes, this will become easier, and I do urge you to carry them with you whenever you can, to keep them by your bedside and to use them as often as possible, especially when you are starting out. This will imprint the physical runes with your energies and make them personal to you, but it will also make them familiar to you and thus more effective.

I personally draw two runes in the morning: one to see what's going on, and one as a sort of message from the Gods, a briefing on what areas I should concentrate on during the day. I would interpret this one slightly differently than the daily 'what's going down?' rune; more as instructions, if you like. So, for example, I might get Berkana, and that will tell me I need to be more kind and nurturing to my friends and family; for everyone I meet that day in fact, more empathetic, perhaps. Or I might get Gebo; to tell me to be more generous, or an Algiz murkstave; to tell me to tread carefully. Ralph Blum, author of the 1982 book, *The Book of Runes*, suggests drawing an evening rune as well, to see how things went during the day, how well you responded to the morning's message, and also gain any feedback. This is a good idea, especially if you follow this practice.

So, let's have a look at the how-to of runecasting. The method used for casting the runes will vary from situation to situation and with individual choice; after all, you might be at home in the privacy of your room or you might be on a train or in a doctor's waiting room when you feel the need of your oracle. Most rune readers will draw at least one rune every morning, to see which way the wind is blowing. My experience is that they speak of the immediate future, and if you want to find out about the distant future or need a more complex question answered, you turn to the Tarot. And, if you have used the Tarot, you are probably familiar with the smaller layouts, such as laying out three cards to represent the past, the current situation and the future – this is an excellent way to start using the runes. You can even progress to using larger Tarot layouts like the classic Celtic Cross, though this is more suited to rune dice (see below), when each stave has more than one chance of being drawn.

To some to some extent, the larger traditional Tarot layouts can also be used, but in general the runes are used for answers to one question or one situation, rather than laid out in an all-encompassing spread as is often the case with the Tarot.

You also need to make some decisions, right at the start of your relationship with the runes: see this as a sort of spiritual pre-nup, if you like. Certain things must be decided between you to rule out misunderstandings. Perhaps the most important one is murkstaves: whether or not you are going to acknowledge these, as not all runemasters do. Will you see runes that have fallen sideways on as murkstaves? This is an apparently trivial question, but in fact very relevant: the runes, like many ancient writing systems, were not necessarily written in the linear, left-to-right manner we write today in English; they could be written from left to right, from right to left, or even as a mixture of the two, with one line going one way and the next going the other, like a Snakes and Ladders board. They were commonly written around the borders of things, sacred stones and images, and you can buy pendants and other jewellery today with this rune border around a pentagram or other pagan symbol; these are called runic wheels.

Another decision to be made is how you will read staves that have fallen in a particular way, perhaps not on the casting cloth, or have even fallen off the table. Murkstaves are one thing, but how do you read runes that have fallen at a sideways angle? At what angle do you consider a rune reversed? This is something you and your runes will have to decide together, as we don't have an owner's manual for them. We don't really know how they were used, and even some of the meanings are academic.

The best way to do this is with a dowsing pendulum. If you use one, you will know that you ask the pendulum each time, 'Show me your 'yes" and 'Show me your 'no" before letting it swing to demonstrate. Using this method, you can easily find out whether murkstaves or fallen staves are to be acknowledged – or you can just make an arbitrary decision about it off the cuff. Just don't go changing your mind about it later on, or changing your mind on a temporary basis because you like the meaning a certain murkstave gives you!

Okay, let's get on and use the runes.

Sit in a quiet place where you will not be disturbed, and ask the blessing and help of any deity you may wish, perhaps including the Norns or even the Allfather himself – he found the runes, after all. It is appropriate to sit facing north, which the Norsemen saw as the direction of the Gods.

Now continue sitting, and think carefully while you play with your runes, running them through your fingers lovingly (which in itself can help to still your mind, just as using a rosary does for people praying) and putting your question into them. It is important not to ask a muddled question (ask a stupid question and you'll get a stupid answer) or change the question halfway through. This might seem a bit 'well, duh!' but it's not easy for our modern minds, with their media-trashed concentration abilities and their crammed multi-tasking agendas, to focus on one job at a time. Sit down to do any spiritual work that requires a bit of time and patience, and your mind suddenly fills up with urgent cries of, 'Did you return So-and-so's call?', 'Did you leave the cooker on?' or 'You were supposed to call the dentist – go on, get up and do it NOW!' Meditators call this annoying internal chatter *Monkey Mind*, and it is the bane of practitioners of any kind of magical or spiritual work. Don't ask me how to sort it without using drugs, but if you do find out – let me know!

Casting Cloths

I personally like to take account of where the runes fall in terms of the cardinal points. Most modern pagans will be familiar with the *correspondences* of the cardinal points, but to quickly sum up: north is home and hearth; east is the mind, career, work; south is health and physical energy; west is

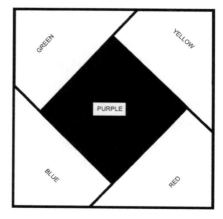

emotion, love and spiritual matters. I mentioned that it is good to have a special cloth to lay the runes on, which will protect them and keep them clean; my clever friend made me a beautiful quilted runecasting cloth which has five different coloured areas, all roughly the same in size: green for north, yellow for east, red for south, blue for west and a purple square in the centre for the spiritual life. It measures 40cms square, a useful size for a casting cloth, though if you commonly throw down onto the ground, you might need a bigger one. The cloth is laid down so that its corners match up with the cardinal points; the green section to the north, the yellow section to the east, etc. I then cast the runes on to the cloth and take note of which runes fall into which area. Maybe I get Algiz in the south, Raido in the centre and Thurisaz in the west. This could be telling me I need to take special care to protect my health, that I need to get off my ass and do more work and make more progress in my spiritual life, and that someone will hurt my feelings with nasty words or actions.

Another idea for a casting cloth or mat is a representation of the nine worlds of Yggdrasil, the worlds of the Gods, of elves and giants, and of men. These could be represented as nine squares stitched together into one larger one, perhaps with their names or a single rune representing their names, sewn into each square or, if you are really clever, a map of Yggdrasil with the nine worlds laid out among its branches. This would be a challenging idea to take on, as the symbolism and meanings of the nine worlds would have to be assimilated before you could start casting the runes on to the cloth. They are:

Asgard: at the top of the tree, Asgard, home of the Aesir Gods, represents deity and the higher self, one's highest spiritual goals.

Liosalfheim: home of the light elves, this realm represents our spirit guides and our path.

Vanaheim: home of the Vanir Gods, this realm is about our fertility and our health, our bodies and our sex lives. It also has connections with the realm of nature and the area of ecology and the environment.

Muspelheim: the home of the fire giants, Muspelheim contains our passions and other strong feelings, the urges that drive us forwards.

Midgard: Midgard is the Earth as we humans know and inhabit it, and is about normal everyday concerns and our relationship to other people.

Niflheim: the realm of fog and ice, is to do with our fantasies and imaginations, and our tendency to get bogged down with them to the exclusion of reality.

Jotunheim: the land of giants is about the primal forces that move us hither and thither, with or without our will; about forces larger than ourselves that we cannot resist.

Svartalfheim: the land of the dark elves is about our own dark urges, perhaps things we have tried to suppress, but they are still there, below the surface, the vices and negative feelings that we cannot get away from.

Hel: the subconscious and deeply buried feelings, perhaps the root of all our behaviours, lie in the realm of the dead at the root of the tree.

This cloth could be used either to cast the runes on randomly, or you could draw the runes one by one, placing one in each realm.

Simple Hand Cast

This is the simplest cast to make other than drawing a single rune. Simply ask your question, then reach into your pouch and draw out a number of runes just as they fall into your hand, in a bunch. Cast them onto a cloth and make your reading. Some will fall on their faces — these are not read — but others may fall reversed, pointing away from you, and these are read as murkstaves. If there is a relationship between two or more runes — they may actually lie against or atop one another — this must be taken into account in the reading.

The Norns (Cast of Three)

Ask your question. Draw three runes, one by one, laying them down in the order in which you draw them and  without turning them at all — remember that a reversed rune, a *murkstave*, has a different meaning. If the runes appear face down, turn them over left to right, not top to bottom, so they keep their orientation.

The first rune represents what has led the querent to this situation, and may be most important in understanding how to change things. The centre rune represents the situation now being experienced, but may have additional information. The last rune, however, does not tell the future... this is not something we do with runes.

The third rune tells of what may result if we continue heedlessly along the path we are on. The future is always perceived as mutable, and the rune reading is carried out as an evaluation process, to bring the querent face to face with how his actions and attitudes have brought about the situation.

Cast of Five

The runes are drawn one by one from the bag and laid out face down in the pattern as illustrated on the right. The three horizontal runes, 2, 1 and 5 represent your past, present and future.

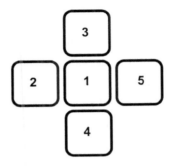

Turn over the centre rune first: this shows your present and your problem as it is now. A negative rune, or one that does not seem relevant can show that the person for whom the reading is being done is agitated and in some trouble.

Rune 2 shows the past that has led to this situation. Rune 3 shows the help you may receive with the situation – a negative or reversed rune here may show reluctance to accept advice or help. Rune 4 speaks of what may be changed about the situation or what must be endured. Rune 5 shows the outcome if all the other factors are taken into consideration.

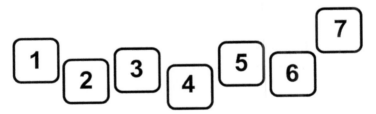

Cast of Seven

A cast of seven is sometimes called the Midgard Serpent (or Jörmungandr), and is then laid out in a wiggly line, instead of as six with one beneath as is often done.

Laying out seven runes allows for more meanings to be seen, and more detail, as there is more than one rune for each factor in your life. This is extremely useful, given the sometimes vague or apparently irrelevant meanings you can receive from them. Lay the runes as before, from left to right, either in the manner of the illustration, or in a line, with the seventh and final one underneath the centre of the row.

The questions you can answer with this layout can be much broader in scope than with some other runecasts. Instead of asking 'yes' or 'no' or 'what about my relationship?', you can ask questions like, 'How will my career improve if I go on this new training course?' or 'If I changed my diet to a lactose-free one, how would this affect my wellbeing?' Through questions like these, you can get enough runic suggestion to help you make all but the toughest decisions.

In this layout, you double up the information received by reading the runes two at a time. Start with numbers one and two, the first two on the left of the cast. These represent the situation you (or your querent) are in, or the problem for which you are asking advice.

Next come staves three and four, which speak of the past and what has led you to the current situation. Staves five and six are next, and these are the most important in the cast, for they are the advice that the runes are giving you; what to do about the situation to achieve a better outcome. They might be about action, or they might be about waiting and taking stock. In each case, because there are two runes to be considered together, read them together, taking note of how they relate to one another and influence one another.

The final stave, rune seven, which in the Jörmundandr layout is the snake's head, is the likely outcome, but bear in mind that this rune will be influenced by the two previous ones, so if you get a very negative rune here and numbers five and six were Sowelu and Fehu, you can relax a bit. It won't be as bad as all that.

This runecast is a bit more complicated, but well worth learning.

Nine Runes Cast

Nine was a deeply magical number to the Norsemen. Pick nine runes at random from the pouch. Hold them between your hands for a moment and focus on your question — holding your fists to your third eye (between and slightly above your eyebrows) is a useful pose for this, or you could hold them to your heart. Then scatter the runes on the table, floor, or cloth, if you have one. Read the runes which land face up first. These will relate to the current situation and the circumstances which led to it. How the runes are read is largely subjective but, in general, runes lying in the centre are the most immediately relevant, while those lying around the edges are less important, or represent more general influences.

As we have seen, runes that are close together or touching often complement each other, giving each other shades of meaning. Sometimes a rune may land directly on top of another, which clearly indicates a divinatory relationship between them. Runes which fall on opposite sides of the pattern frequently show opposing influences. Occasionally, a rune will land completely off the cloth or fall off the table. Some people consider such runes to be particularly significant, while others ignore them completely.

First look at the runes which landed face up, then turn over the runes that landed face downwards, without moving them from their positions and without changing their orientation (unless you have decided to ignore murkstaves). These represent outside or future influences. This more complex spread will give you many shades of meaning.

Rune Dice

This elegant system is relatively new in the timeline of runes, but they work in much the same way as the individual staves, and are very compact to carry around, as they will fit in a tiny pouch. They can be bought ready-made, but they are easy to make as well, as long as you can source some little wooden cubes – about the size of sugar cubes would be the size you would need (and I just checked, and you can buy beautifully finished blank dice on sites like Etsy). You only need five, as four of the dice will contain all the 24 runes, six to a die, and the fifth represents Wyrd, so has one blank side and a dot or other non-rune mark on the others. You may decide you don't need the Wyrd die, as this equates to the blank rune found in some sets, which is meaningless. Draw the rune symbols onto the dice faces until you have them all — it really doesn't matter which rune goes on which surface, as they will all be selected randomly or thrown like gaming dice.

Some people even use a special dice cup for these, but you can just shake them in your hand and drop one out of your fingers to see which side lands uppermost or drop one die blind into your other hand and roll it. Then you write it down, replace the dropped die with the others and shake and repeat until you have a full reading of three or more dice, depending on which of the runecasts you are using.

Rune Cards

It is also possible to buy runes as cards, which are easier to handle, for example, on a moving train or in a plane, especially one that has just hit some turbulence, as the cards are dealt and laid out like any other cards. I can see that these would have their uses, but they wouldn't really replace three-dimensional runes. They might be good for beginners, to help them learn the runes and their meanings, as some of the sets you can buy have information about each rune on the card face.

Ground Casting and Rune Scrying

Some rune readers, rather than using a cloth or a tabletop, throw their runes directly on the ground. As you may not want to disrespect your primary set by tossing them on the ground in this manner but would still like to be able to do this at outdoor venues, you can use small twigs or those wooden lolly-sticks (which you can buy in some supermarkets or online in bulk — or just eat a lot of lollies) for this. Inscribe them with the rune symbols. All 24 are then thrown down onto the ground and read as they lie. Runes lying face down are ignored. If two runes are touching or lying close together, they are then seen as influencing one another. A light trance state is best for reading this kind of cast, as there is no 'geography' for the way the runes lie. Again, as with scrying with many items like rune stones, it is generally accepted that the runes at the centre are the most important and those further away are less important.

Runecasting for others

In some ways, runes are handier than Tarot cards, as they pop up with a simple message and don't need years of study before you can wring some meaning from a cast. There will come a time when you feel pretty confident about your ability to read the runes, and other people will start asking you to do casts for them over simple problems, and maybe later, not-so-simple ones.

The method is the same, except that your friend should handle the runes if possible, putting his or her question into them just as you do, before they are cast. Make sure they take their time over this, just as you would yourself; explain to them that a rushed, careless questioning of the runes will lead to a muddled and confusing answer. This will not always be possible, of course, if your friend lives a long way off, or is even in another country, but it is easy enough to do rune reading by telephone and email. Think hard of your friend as you handle the runes and ask their question. You can even have a photograph of your friend placed in the centre of the runecasting cloth, and obviously then take note of which runes lie closest to his image, as these will be the most important in the reading.

You can also photograph the runes as they lie to include in the email with your reading, or to show to them in a video chat.

And of course, you can achieve a face to face reading with online platforms like Zoom, Messenger and WhatsApp. Your querent could then even select his or her own runes, by drawing from a pack of rune cards at their end of the broadband fibre. You could even have mailed them a homemade pack of cards with simply drawn runes for the purpose.

Worried about a friend who is sick or in trouble? Rather than rushing to the phone at some inconvenient time, and perhaps dragging them out of their sickbed, draw a single rune for a quick update on how they are doing, until you can speak to them properly.

Sometimes it is as though the runes become more proactive themselves, as you get to know them better. You will start to have the experience of seeing them pop up in Nature or other places and will get used to these small messages happening. The runes are simple signs and they do appear everywhere: twigs, marks on the grass, flames, airplane trails and bird flights in the sky, man-made signs, cracks in the paving… The list goes on. If you are attuned to your runes, you will find that you see these phenomena more and more. If you get one that you don't understand, draw a rune when you get home to see what it is about (or right there and then if you carry the runes with you), but mostly you will find the message is very quickly followed up by what it was telling you about.

Using a dowsing pendulum with the runes can also help with clarification. If you have drawn a rune you don't understand, try dowsing over it with suggestions: 'Is this about my new job offer?', 'Is this to do with the quarrel I had with my sister?' In my experience, the runes work well with another medium like this, which is useful as they do not give the depth of message you might get from, say, Tarot or the I-Ching.

Finished with your divinatory work? Thank the runes (or the rune dice) before putting them away, and if someone else has handled them; perhaps to ask a question before casting, you can cleanse them with sage smoke, with intention, with moonlight or even with a dash of spray polish and a soft cloth. Don't worry too much: they know they are yours and will not usually retain imprints from other people's auric bodies.

CHAPTER SIX

Spelling it Out

Nothing is inherently magical. Not crystals, not herbs, not symbols, not graveyard dirt dug from a hanged man's grave with John Dee's own monogrammed trowel at midnight. The magic comes from you and through you from the Gods. Magical sigils work because you have focused on them to create them and put your will and belief into them. Terry Pratchett fans will recognise this phenomenon as '*headology*' – people think you're a witch and you can do magic because you wear a pointy hat, and the pointy hat is a witch's hat because you wear it. I think I feel one of my heads coming on, but the essence is that magic works because you expect it to, because you *know it will*.

And yet, please ignore what I have just said about nothing being magical, as it is vital you believe in the crystals, the herbs, the sigils and the grave dust if you are to succeed as a magical practitioner... magic is all about belief, and primarily belief in yourself and the tools and substances you have assembled to aid you. And sigils, whether they are traditional symbols like the runes or something that you have cooked up yourself from a statement of magical intent, are one of the most useful and versatile items in a witch's bag of tricks.

The next consideration is the ethics... should you do this? (And I'm not invoking any biblical '*Thou shalt not suffer a witch to live*' notions here, just stating fact.) Magic works, and if you are careless with it, it will work in ways you do not expect or desire. Sometimes you may even receive a warning that what you want is not something that you should be doing magic for. Always examine your own feelings, for there will be times when you feel uneasy or reluctant to set up and perform magic for a particular reason. When it comes to performing magic for others – which you should ideally do only at their request – the same ideas pertain.

A friend asked me to help her son, who had tried to get into the police and been rejected, and now wanted to join the fire service. I didn't want to do it: all I could think of, as I tinkered with my tools and put them away again, was of Mark[7] burned, trapped in a blazing building, suffocated with toxic smoke. So, I didn't do it and Mark, who may have asked for help because he didn't want to do something about the fact that he was overweight and unfit, didn't get the job, but my conscience was clear.

So, think carefully before you engage in magical practice, especially if you are planning to work for someone else.

Whether the runes were designed for divination and later found to be an excellent magical tool, or whether it was the reverse, is not really known, but they were an integral part of Seidr, the Norse magical tradition. Seidr (pronounced like the drink), which was the concern of Freyja, Goddess of Witches, was about both seeing and 'tweaking' the future by means of enchantments, including chanting spells, shamanism and possibly acts of sex magic. Rune magicians, or *Vitkar*, specialised in using the runes for magic as sigils, or in other ways which we will examine later on.

The runes were a magical tool accessible to everyone, even those who could not read or write – provided that they could at least recognise which runes were which (and Norse tradition includes warning tales about those who used the runes without understanding them properly – a little knowledge is a dangerous

---

7   Name changed for the purpose of this narrative.

thing!). Their name translates as 'hidden' or 'secret', which clearly shows they were used for magical practices and probably that the knowledge of their meanings and how to use them was originally confined to a class of magicians or shamans.

The commonest use of the runes was as simple charms or amulets; perhaps carried on the person or worn as jewellery, carved on weapons, for example, to keep their bearer safe and make them victorious in battle, on cradles to protect the baby, on lintels, doors and doorposts to protect the home and bring prosperity – much as pagans would use them today, although we might also place them in our cars and on our IT devices and phones as well. Runes were carved on pieces of bone or scraps of leather and laid under a sick person's bed to heal them, or carefully scribed in a spell to gain someone's love. They were carved on stables and cowsheds, or maybe even tied around an ailing animal's neck, to help stock stay healthy and fertile. And just as we thank our Gods for successful magical outcomes, so no doubt the Norsemen would have made a sacrifice – or *blót* – to thank their deities for charms that worked as they were intended.

So, let's start looking through the various ways runes can be used in magical work.

Charms, Amulets and Talismans

In case you are not aware of the different meanings of these terms, I will just clarify. An amulet is a magical item carried for protection against bad luck or danger, a talisman is a lucky charm carried for a specific purpose, eg. for success in an exam or in business, while a charm is just that: an item carried to attract good luck generally. As examples: a Christian cross, worn to protect one from evil spirits, is an amulet. A lucky cigarette lighter, carried by a card player who believes it brings him luck at the card table, is a talisman. And a pretty brooch in the shape of a four-leafed clover, or one of those gruesome rabbits' feet, worn 'because it's lucky', is a charm.

All these things may consist of or include gemstones, slips of paper with writing, pieces of biological material such as bones, feathers and claws, sigils or images made into jewellery and small bags of magical items such as herbs, gems and written spells. Runes lend themselves very well to being used in this way, as they are easy to inscribe on a piece of wood for use as a pendant – in fact runic jewellery of all kinds is readily available these days – or on a slip of wood or paper to go into a charm bag.

Just to give you some examples, we will have a quick visit with our old friends Leif and Jayden to see the uses they make of the runes in terms of charms, amulets and talismans.

Leif has Algiz, the rune of protection, probably the most useful of all the runes, over the lintel of his timber-and-lath farmhouse, as well as over the cowshed, goat shed and pigsties. These are lawless times, and even landowners like Leif may suffer at the hands of ruffians marauding for what they can carry off: livestock, goods or even Leif's pretty wife. Inside his home, he also has this daddy of all protective runes carved in various places, and Frida has had him carve it into the cradle, so that each child in turn is protected, when tiny and vulnerable during the first few months of life.

In various other places, as well as over the family shrine, hangs Fehu, the rune of prosperity and the God Freyr's own rune – remember, Freyr is Leif's personal deity – made from plaited straw. This is renewed at each harvest with due ceremony and offerings of beer, mead and pork (Freyr's sacred animal). Leif himself wears the rune Fehu on a leather disc on a thong around his neck, to keep him in mind of his personal deity and to bring him luck in his work and his life generally. Frida does not use runes herself, but a crude doll-like image of Frigga sits within the shrine as well, the Goddess to whom she prays. Frigga's area of influence, as you recall, is the home and children, so she is especially close to Frida's heart.

In the stable, old Svartfaxi is also protected with the runes Algiz and Ehwaz on the door and walls, also inscribed on wooden discs hung from his tack.

Jayden has bindrunes incorporating Algiz around his home, as there has been a spate of burglaries on the estate recently, and he is concerned. Across the threshold – and Jayden, as a neopagan, is aware of the magical significance of this area – he has recently laid a strip of card with the rune Thurisaz inscribed across it nine times with the point facing the outside, hidden under the doormat. In his car a fluffy bear hangs from the mirror – something his work colleagues teased him about, so he told them Amber put it there as a joke – but the bear has the protective and lucky runes Algiz, Raido and Ehwaz drawn on a segment of ribbon it holds almost hidden between its paws. Jayden has also drawn protective runes on the car's logbook in charged water, which of course is invisible once it has dried. His smartphone has tiny protective runes drawn on inconspicuously in dark enamel, as does his laptop, and in his cubicle at work there is more evidence of his pagan beliefs... for those who know what to look for. At home he has a small shrine to Odin on a shelf and offers a drop of beer in the evenings when he is relaxing with a drink himself, or a glass of scotch on special festivals. Amber isn't allowed to interfere with it; Jayden doesn't think for a moment Odin would appreciate flowers, which would be Amber's girly first choice of offering, and anyway, she's not a pagan.

Sigils and Bindrunes

Sacred alphabets have always been an important item in magicians' and witches' tool kits, from the beauty of the Ancient Egyptian hieroglyphs, which were held to be magical in their own right, to the use of Klingon in magical workings by Trekkie pagans today (and why not?). Again, *headology* plays a vital part in the use of these scripts, whether they be ancient Babylonian cuneiform or an alphabet you made up on the back of an envelope. I have successfully used Tolkien's runic alphabet Cirth – which he devised himself for his works of fiction – in magic.

The word sigil simply means a magical symbol of any kind, but specifically refers to symbols created by tying letters together to make a new and more complex shape. The system was pioneered by the 19th – 20th century occultist Austin Osman Spare, who wrote down magical intentions in a brief sentence using ordinary English/Latin letters, and then condensed down the letters until he had only one of each kind. These were then designed together into a fantastical pattern, hardly discernible as being made from letters at all, and used as the focus for magical workings. To give an example of an ordinary English alphabet sigil, here is one I designed for my students. Its intention is: 'make the neighbour's cat stop crapping on my vegetable plot', and you can see the C for cat (or crap) is central to the finished motif. Runes are equally useful in this discipline, and in fact are rather easier, as they are all straight lines, so are much less trouble to draw.

Sigils really entered the Tech Age recently, when an app called Sigilengine was launched, for technopagans to generate their own sigils on a computer. It creates very neat and beautiful sigils effortlessly, using a sigil wheel method, but I can't help feeling that it rather disregards the whole point of them, which is to focus the brain. Still, in a culture where a ten-minute YouTube video is too long to sit through and people want things done yesterday, this too has its place, I guess. The app works by asking you to enter your intention, and then does all the boring part of the work, removing surplus letters and finally delivering a sexy looking sigil which you can print off. It doesn't seem to cope with runes yet, though.

Runes are not only used singly as sigils, but two or more runes are often combined to create a more complex sigil called a bindrune. The Norsemen do not seem to have used bindrunes as we do today, but they did tie lines of runes together in vertical or horizontal lines or strings, which worked the same way.

Bindrunes are an easy and versatile way of focusing magical intent, and of carrying it with you or placing it within a charm bag or witch bottle. Some magical people design a bindrune of their name to use on their magical utensils and papers; I use mine on ritual scripts to stop my copy getting mixed up with someone else's.

To give an example: I wish to send healing to my friend who is ill. The best rune for healing is Sowelu, but I will add Algiz for protection against the illness and Berkana for healing and nurturing. Then I will add Kenaz which, as well as being a healing rune, has the power to strengthen the spell.

The runes are tied together in the manner of this example using the Goddess name Aradia (*right*):

As you can see, the result is a tidy little symbol which can be used in any way you like. The aim is to have it as compact as possible, while still including every component of the original rune choices. It is completely okay to turn them around; the Norsemen wrote their runes from left to right or from right to left, as the fancy took them. If this isn't possible, you can make

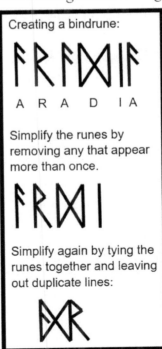

Creating a bindrune:

A R A D I A

Simplify the runes by removing any that appear more than once.

Simplify again by tying the runes together and leaving out duplicate lines:

them into other shapes, squares, triangles and wheels, with the component runes stuck in at artistic angles, or string them along lines as the Norsemen would have done. You can deliberately shape the bindrune with the purpose of the spell in mind: aim for a round shape, perhaps, if you are hoping for protection or luck in travel or make a square shape if your magic is aimed at your home. The symbol is charged in any way you like, with inchantment[8], with a crystal wand, or just with focus and intent.

Bindrunes are an incredibly useful part of a practitioner's array and to this can be added bindrunes that have been created by other people. Probably the best-known examples are the two quite similar protective bindrunes Aegishjalmur[9] (*above*) and Vegvisir (*below*), both examples of a wheel bindrune. These were used historically for protection, Aegishjalmur in battle and Vegvisir in travel.

Although best known as a warrior's protective sigil, Aegishjalmur works for any kind of protection and I had it stuck up all over my house during the Covid crisis and have used it for many different kinds of protection generally. Vegvisir might work better on your car, and specifically on your SatNav device.

Single runes are also useful in magical workings and can be added to the altar or other working space when you are creating a spell. At the end of this chapter, you will find an index advising which runes go with which kinds of magic. As I mentioned earlier, you can acquire larger wooden discs for the altar, and inscribe a

8   Not a spelling error: to inchant is to sing or chant magical words over an item to charge it with magical intent.
9   Pronounced Ag-ish-YAL-moor.

rune or bindrune on these as part of the set-up. A piece of paper or card would serve the same purpose, or even a ceramic tile or plate, which could be wiped clean after the working, ready for the next time. Or you can use a rune board, which can then be left on the altar until the working has achieved its purpose. If using a reusable medium such as a rune board, it is advisable to cleanse it between workings, so that energies are not carried over from one piece of spellcraft to another. This is easily done by smudging with sage smoke or, if there is time before the next need for it, leaving it on a windowsill to be cleansed by the Full Moon.

Written Spells

One of the easiest ways of casting a spell is by simple writing; it works in the same way as magical affirmations, and often just copying the words you have composed, perhaps several times, can be a powerful magical method. The Norsemen might have copied the runes nine times, as that was a most magical number to them; modern pagans might use three, nine or 13. Writing that same affirmation with an alien alphabet such as runes can be even more effective. Because the runes are not your own cultural letters, you are forced to adopt a different brain rhythm while converting your words into runic, which can manifest as a light trance. Magical practitioners are familiar with this condition and utilise it deliberately, as they have found it to be a necessary part of magical workings.

One easy way of enhancing the power of runes used this way is by investing in an ink pen, perhaps a feathered Harry Potter-style quill pen – easily found in magic shops and online these days – and some posh-looking parchment paper. These kinds of elements bring a sense of *fun* to your work, which is actually quite important in making your magic effective. Don't forget that your imagination, as well as your will, is vital in effective magic, and needs to be activated.

An additional technique is to then concentrate on the sigil you have produced, putting all your powers of will and intent into it for as long as you can. This is best done with a written copy of the sigil, perhaps on your rune board or a piece of card. A traditional pose for this is to splay your hands so the thumbs are at right angles to the fingers, thus forming a square enclosure with your hands, which is placed around the sigil while you stare at it and inchant whatever verbal component you have designed for the spell. There are various breathing exercises that can help with this, and mental postures that will help activate the sigil; but here, as any witch will tell you, a strong and vivid visualisation of the desired outcome is worth ten of that. If you are rubbish at visualisation (and many of us are, thanks to hours of televising), you can substitute an affirmation, a muttered repetition of the desired outcome. This is always spoken in a positive way, as magic will see any negative statement as a positive one. If, for example, you don't want your partner to be in a bad mood when you get home, do *not* say, 'My partner will not be in a bad mood this evening,' as this will be heard by the mechanics of magic as what you actually want. Instead, make the statement positive: 'My partner will be in a good mood tonight.'

Once the spell is finished, walk away. Go and watch some mindless television, eat some junk food, have a cup of tea and scratch your armpits, or whatever other part of your anatomy suggests itself. I'm not actually being facetious here: it is important to remove yourself and your reawakening Monkey Mind from the vicinity of the spell, to take your attention from it and let it do its work. I usually explain this to my students as avoiding opening the oven door every few minutes to see if your cake is rising – because it certainly won't if you do that.

There are more 'magical' ways of doing this grounding work, taking you away from the scene of the crime by meditation, visualisation or other exercises, and there are more unusual methods, such as ritual laughter, which involves a burst of mirthless artificial laughter to shift the mind into another space. The recent trend for 'laughter yoga' is perhaps related to this: laughter has powers we still do not fully appreciate. I know practitioners who go outside and walk on the earth in bare feet, but this rather depends on the weather at the time.

The runes or other letters you have used can be pinned up over your magical working space, or anywhere else in your home, or carried on your person, perhaps in your wallet or handbag or laptop case; until they have achieved what you set out to do. When you have finished, the paper you have used can then be ritually disposed of, perhaps burned, dropped into running water, thrown into the winds, or buried in the earth. It is not good to do this in an area that is environmentally sensitive, but you can use a medium that is naturally quickly biodegradable, such as rice paper. I keep a spell box – which does not have to be an intricately carved or special box at all, a biscuit tin will do the job just as well. Flammable material from spellworkings is placed in here, written inchantments, photographs of people needing healing, poppets and wooden or paper runes and sigils; accumulating all year, then burned ritually at some notable date, such as Samhain or Yule, when you might have a fire in your hearth.

In a ritual situation, spells can be written on magician's flash paper, easily obtainable online, which is then flashed over the cauldron by someone who knows what they are doing, which should make everybody gasp with surprise. Or you can use a reusable item such as a rune board or tile, or even write the runes on your skin with a soft felt pen. Spells written for healing or other workings for others can be given or sent to them (assuming they know that you are a magical practitioner and that you are doing magic for them), for them to keep until they feel better. This can also be done with candles, a vital part of any magical practitioner's toolkit, and chosen with regard to their colour, as certain colours are seen as necessary for certain types of spells in modern magic. Runes can be inscribed on the candles, which are then burned as part of the larger working or can be sent to the person for whom the magic has been done.

Many practitioners have tattoos of runes and bindrunes, and perhaps believe that having, say Fehu and Algiz on their shoulder will ensure they lead a carefree life. I'm not sure about this one. Familiarity breeds contempt, and how can a sigil that snuggles up to your underwear and is bathed in your sweat be very magical? At least with jewellery you must make a conscious effort to wear it, and to keep it clean and shiny. But perhaps I'm just showing my age.

Whilst runes work very well on their own, they also tie in quite happily with other magical methods and can be popped onto a crystal grid or carved on a candle or burned in the cauldron, or the ink washed from the paper or tile into a potion... and I'm sure you have plenty more suggestions.

One idea from the Norsemen's own historical practice is a *nidstang* or curse pole. Long before Mario Puzo had the idea of leaving a disembodied horse head in his character's bed in *The Godfather*, the Norsemen would use the head to top a long pole, facing towards the home of the person they wanted to curse, and with what they wanted to happen to the enemy carved in runes down the pole. Often the horse's skin and other parts were added to this gruesome artefact. Don't try this at home.

Numerology of Runes

Witches and other magical practitioners use numerology a fair amount, and it can be applied to runes, just as to any alphabet. Numerology works like this: each letter of the alphabet is assigned a value. In our Latin-English letters it runs like this: a = 1, b = 2, c = 3, until you get to 9; then it starts again, so that i = 9, but j = 1. A word can thus be turned into numbers like this: *spell* = s(1) + p(7) + e(5) + l(3) + l(3) = 19. If the resulting sum has more than one number it is condensed down again: 1 + 9 = 10, and again: 1 + 0 = 1. This is also done with actual numbers, so a birth date can be reduced to one figure as well. This number is then related to the magical order of planets (which in astrology includes the Sun and Moon), with the Sun at number 1, the Moon at number 2, Mercury (or Jupiter, depending on which system you use) at number 3, and so on, and many practitioners will regard this number as important to them as their astrological birth sign, and ensure any magical name they take also tots up to this number, tweaking it where necessary to ensure it does.

The runes have numbers from one to 24 assigned to them (see Chapter Four), but after that the method is just the same. When creating a magical mantra or rune string, it is considered advantageous to ensure the numerology adds up to a significant number, as this will further empower the spell.

The Norsemen had their own system of magical numbers, with nine being considered the most powerful, as it represented the nine worlds of the Cosmos; so a rune string or chant that adds up to nine would be considered the most powerful. Three is also a significant number: there are three Norns, Yggdrasil has three taproots, Odin was one of three brothers, and so on. Eight is also significant, as there are eight Otherworlds (the nine worlds of Yggdrasil minus Midgard, on which we live).

The number can also be aligned back to one of the runes, by ensuring your spell or rune string condenses down to the number of the rune you wish to use. For example, a spell for protection should condense to 15, the number of the protection rune Algiz, and a spell for healing to 17 (Berkana) or 16 (Sowelu). Yes, you have spotted the problem with this idea, but I must remind you that intent is everything in magic, so if you want to align to Algiz and not Kenaz, you just stop condensing at 15, or compose your chant of two words and deal with them separately.

Runes to use for specific purposes

CONFIDENCE:	Ansuz, Sowelu, Daggaz
ENDURANCE AND STRENGTH:	Thurisaz, Uruz, Teiwaz, Ehwaz, Hagalaz
HEALING:	Sowelu, Berkana, Kenaz, Ingwaz
INSPIRATION:	Ansuz, Daggaz, Laguz, Kenaz
LUCK:	Fehu, Sowelu, Wunjo, Jera
NEW BEGINNINGS AND INITIATIONS:	Berkana, Eiwaz, Uruz, Daggaz
PROSPERITY:	Fehu, Jera, Sowelu,
PROTECTION:	Algiz, Thurisaz, Raido and Ehwaz (both specifically for protection in travel), Berkana (especially for children)
ROMANCE:	Ingwaz, Wunjo, Kenaz
SUCCESS:	Jera, Sowelu, Wunjo, Teiwaz

You will note that not all the runes appear in this list, but it is far from complete, and there may well be magical uses for the ones I have omitted.

To give a couple of simple examples: I might use Fehu and Jera while planting out my garden vegetables, written onto a small plant label and tucked out of sight among the seedlings, or simply drawn in the earth. For protection on a long car journey, I might use Algiz (always Algiz for protection – it should be a Pavlovian response to this word) with Raido, and Ehwaz to influence the car not to break down! Don't forget that it is magical intent that drives the rune sigils; don't just draw 'em on with a Sharpie and expect them to work without putting some intent and ceremony into the drawing.

I think I'm written out on this subject, so let's go and have a look at runes in other forms.

CHAPTER SEVEN

Words of Wisdom

Inchantments, the spoken component of spells, are a vital part of spellcraft, and have been since our ancient ancestors gathered around sacred hills and standing stones to watch the tribal priests and shamans perform their work to bring a steady flow of game and tall crops. This was long before our ancestors developed a literate culture, and in some cases their beliefs would have prevented them from writing down sacred matters, so such lore would have been passed from priest to priest down the generations by word of mouth. And in more recent times, we know that the Norsemen used spoken magic, but was that based on their runes?

The Norsemen were a fairly literate people, it is believed, and men and women of all classes used the runes for writing and for magic and divination. Yet the use and understanding of writing is so deeply linked in with the spoken language areas of the brain that readers clearly hear in their minds the sound of the words they are reading from a page, and some who are less book-learned may move their lips to help their thought processes while reading or writing. It is difficult to believe that the Norsemen would utilise the runes purely as carvings or writings, especially as they had given these letters such beautiful and resounding names. Would not each rune come to represent the qualities it predicted, becoming in the end a magical incantation to bring about the realisation of its meaning?

As well as the spoken names of the runes, it is likely that the old runemasters used incantations to the runes, to coax them to put forth their secrets. This is not unusual with tools of divination, from the words that may be addressed by a modern witch to her crystal globe or scrying mirror, to the traditional little rhyme spoken to the witch's runes: *'Stones a-Leary, stones a-Leary, tell me truly, tell me clearly...'*

A short prose or verse invocation to Odin, as master of the runes, or to Freyja, mistress of magic, might well have been the habit of the runemasters before they drew forth their rune pouches and cast the staves, and probably also afterwards, to thank deity and the runes themselves, for their gift of enlightenment.

Spoken magic, which the Norsemen called *Galdr*, was so well developed within this culture that they even had a special poetic metre for magical work, called *Galdralag*, loosely translated as 'spell metre', which was kept exclusively for spells and charms and never used for ordinary verse.

Norse poetry was quite different to what we consider poetry today; it did not rhyme, for one thing, and the main components that marked it out as poetry were alliteration and synonyms, which included kennings. The usual form of verse known as *Ljodahattra* was made up of six lines. Lines one and two were matched together with alliteration, line three stood alone, then came another two lines tied together with alliteration, and a final line which stood alone, a form of verse which seems to have more in common with our modern limerick than with what we might consider serious verse today.

Thus a (very rough) modern imitation might read something like this:

> *Hairy Harald hefted his heavy hammer,*
> *Hit his hated hinderer on the head,*
> *Spilled his blood on the earth.*

Went on his way willingly and well,
Nor would he wait to watch the wretch's wane,
Never shall he rise again.

As you can see, I have beaten the alliteration to death, but the rules only called for one word in each paired line to begin with the same letter, although more was fine. Although consonants had to be the same for alliteration, all vowels were considered the same sound, so that two words beginning with 'A' and 'O', for example, would be considered alliteration. The rune poems were probably originally meant to be chanted or even sung, as a way of memorising and passing on their information and, with their alliteration and simple rhythm, would have sounded very impressive.

Galdralag, while adhering to this rule in outline, has additional lines added for emphasis, just as we might repeat magical chants today to reinforce our magical will. These would be added as lines 7 and 8 and might also be tied together with alliteration. Here is an example of a modern English spell using Galdralag which I used for a friend who was unwell for several weeks with long Covid:

Blessings on my fair-faced friend
Fallen and faint with a fever,
Healing I send to her.
May she rise up smiling and strong,
And shine in my sight, sound as ever
And go about her daily life,
And bloom in hearty health
And be herself and happy.

The 'And…' construction at the beginning of the lines is typical of Norse verse.

Usually, I find it easier to keep magical chants, or inchantments, to a simple rhyming couplet, especially if you need to repeat them over and over again, unless you want to end up with your tongue in a splint. But many practitioners will feel that using the original verse forms used by the Norsemen for galdr will add something to their work, even if they compose the verse in modern English. Adding the names of runes to the verse will be a useful way of bringing their power into the spell, especially if their images are already being used in the magical working space.

Spoken Runes

The first problem that may occur to you as you consider this method of working with them is the pronunciation. Their names are rooted in another time, another culture and another language, which used different methods of pronouncing letters than we do today. I have given you a rough guide to pronouncing each name in Chapter Two, but if you feel in need of more confidence with these names, there are plenty of websites that have audio pronunciation help, although they don't always agree and can't all be relied on. I can recommend Professor Jackson Crawford's posts on YouTube; he is an American linguist specialising in Old Norse and, although he has no interest in the magical or divinatory use of runes, he is helpful with how to speak their names.

Some rune readers find the rune names fascinating and learn their pronunciations correctly, trying with huge relish to recite them as closely as possible to how they would have been spoken in the original Norse. To be honest though, if you find all this hard to cope with: pronounce them in the way that seems best to you. Magic comes from you in the first place, and you know what you are talking about. The same is also true of deity: plenty of ancient deities must now answer to modern versions of their names. For example, I would point out that Kemetics (an example of bad etymology) through the decades since the movement's founding, have referred to their major Goddess as Isis, the Greek form of her name; her real name being something like A-*gasp*-set, and that this does not seem to have affected their relationship with her.

A single rune name can be spoken like a mantra, as an affirmation or inchantment, or you can take two or more rune names and turn them into a chant for spell casting or incorporate them into a rhymed verse with other words. These, in a combination including visualisation, drumming, gestures and motions, can form a very effective way of working, either with or without the full magical altar set-up. The Norsemen seem to have used the runes in a very much simpler manner, with some examples having been found of runic inscriptions that include apparently meaningless repetitions of one or more runes in a string. Scholars believe these may have been runic spells. In the examples I have seen, it is the rune *sound* that is incorporated into the chants, not its name, so that Ansuz-Mannaz-Ansuz (perhaps a charm for spreading information or inspiration through the tribe?) becomes AMAMA. Imagine how effective this could be, repeated as a mantra with magical drumming, in a dim but candle-lit room with incense smoke swirling about you as you concentrate on your task. It could easily be imagined being performed by Norse-inspired musical groups like Heilung. Mystics have long been aware that repetitions, even of meaningless sounds, alter the brainwave patterns, which as we know is one of the things that has to happen with magic.

The letters Ansuz, Laguz, Uruz also appear quite commonly as a string, making the word ALU, and it is believed this may have been a reference to a *blót*, or offering, and that perhaps the very mention of the rune names in this manner served as an actual offering. This is far from unprecedented: the best-known historic example may be the tomb art of the Ancient Egyptians, which often portrayed meat, bread, fruit and wine, in the belief that the dead person could actually eat these things because he or she had their images, or even just the mention of their names in writing.

So as an example, let's do some weather magic using a single rune name as a mantra. You want a warm day to meet your friend for a walk on the beach or in the park. You haven't seen them for a long time, thanks to Covid restrictions, and this is important to you. Put that importance into your actions, as you draw Sowelu on a tile or piece of wood and charge it with your wand. So-wel-u has three syllables, and the stave is composed of three strokes, so it is easy to simply inchant the name in time as you draw the symbol again and again over your workspace or on your tile or rune board, meanwhile filling your head with images as vivid as you can manage of a sunny day and your friend and yourself in summery shorts and T-shirts. The chant of 'So-wel-u So-wel-u So-wel-u' can be repeated as often as you like with the images you conjured up; remember, will and visualisation are the heart of magic, along with the change in brainwave rhythm that such chanting can bring about. If you wanted to add a bit more bang to the spell, you could add another rune, perhaps Wunjo for the joy of meeting your friend. Then you would abbreviate the rune names to their actual sounds and make the chant something like SOVOSOVO. I've done this sort of work and it can work like.... a charm!

The names of some runes can be muttered under one's breath in a public place and attract no more attention than the absent-minded chewing of one's lip. Many people have nervous facial habits such as lip-biting, excessive blinking and teeth grinding, so that minor movement of the lips will hardly be noticed by anyone else — unless they happen to be deaf! Some of the more sibilant rune names or those that do not necessitate opening the lips very wide to enunciate them, such as Fehu, Raido and Teiwaz can be used inaudibly without anyone noticing. If you need to do this kind of work in a public place and feel you might attract attention, simply whip out your phone: no one takes any notice of a person muttering at or to their phone, especially if you have a pair of ear buds in place. And remember: the Gods are not deaf, they do not require you to shout at them or *vibrate* their names, or even speak aloud at all. You are a part of them, and they can hear every thought in your head.

Music and song would no doubt have played an important role in both religious ritual and magic, as it does for neopagans today, and probably in a very commonplace, day-to-day manner. When you reflect that as late as the second half of the 20th century, it was common to hear adults and children of both sexes humming, whistling and singing aloud in the street or at work, you realise how much recorded media has taken away from us, and how it has helped to extinguish traditional folk and popular songs and children's playground chants, relegating them to the territory of specialised folk music organisations. Going back a little further, you would have found milkmaids singing traditional songs or chants they knew would relax the cows and raise their yields, farmers' wives singing charms to help the hens lay and themselves to find the eggs, dairymaids singing songs to make the butter 'come' in the churn, ploughboys singing charms to help the horses pull the ploughshare through hard soil and fishermen singing charms to bring good weather and large catches. Some little ditties we know from early childhood may have had their beginnings in charms of this kind, for example the nursery rhyme, *'Rain, rain, go away; come again another day'* which dates back in written form to the 17th century, but may well be many centuries older and is clearly a weather charm.

In Finland, a fascinating and beautiful custom called rune singing has continued to the present day, with rune songs about every aspect of life from cycling to making a cup of tea. This use of the word rune has nothing to do with Norse runes: the Finnish language is not related to Norse, and the word comes from the word for part of a horse's bridle, which shows that at least some of the songs were originally descended from horse charms. But it is also associated with the magical decoration of musical instruments with rune-like signs. It is clearly a very ancient art form, and perhaps started life as a way of handing on knowledge and ritual in a non-literate culture, and a way of handing down stories and other traditions. The songs may have begun life as chanted songs to stop the rain, to ease childbirth, to ensure a good catch of fish, to attract deer and other game. Every culture has or has had spoken or sung charms like this, used by all the people to ensure the safety, health and success of their families and their own endeavours. I have mentioned the probable origin of some of our now vanishing children's nursery rhymes and playground songs, but many of our traditional folk songs may have originated in this way. Incidentally, I am indebted to Dr Anna-Elena Pääkkölä of Turku University, not only for her help with this section, but for the information that Tolkien was well acquainted with Finnish folklore and legends, and incorporated many of their ideas into his fiction, especially *The Silmarillion*.

Using Norse runes in this way is not only following in an ancient tradition, but a good way of reinforcing your knowledge of the runes and how they work. While the child with a basket in a farmyard of the past might have called out a traditional chicken song, encouraging the hen to 'lay an egg for my tea' with a plain magical purpose, it would be easy enough to compose your own simple chants using rune names or sounds for everyday good luck or purposes. Here are a few to get you started:

> *Laguz, rune of lakes and streams,*
> *Bring me sleep and pleasant dreams.*

This might be useful to someone who habitually suffers from insomnia, for example. Or:

> *Teiwaz take away my fear,*
> *Make me brave and strong as Tyr.*

When courage is needed for anything, such as facing a new boss or mother-in-law. Or:

O Berkana, Lady of the Trees,
Heal my friend and bring him ease.

And finally, to the most useful rune of all, a charm to Algiz for protection, easily learned and easily muttered:

I take Algiz as my shield,
All this day its power I wield,
From all perils I am sealed.

Another way of using the runes in chanting is to make words or even short sentences with the runes you are using, which can then be used as an inchantment or mantra. If, for example, you wished to protect yourself while travelling, you might take the runes Algiz, Raido and Ehwaz. Reciting the names of these runes would work well, but all three rune names would be a bit cumbrous, and the sounds alone run off the tongue more easily. They are Z, R and E, which don't easily make up a chantable word. But of course, you can use each rune sound more than once, so this then becomes ZEREZ. A little experimentation will teach you which runes work well in this way and which sound best or roll off the tongue more easily. It may sound a bit daft, but this repetition does, as I have said before, alter brainwave patterns, and this is what you are trying to achieve here, in order to manifest your magical will.

CHAPTER EIGHT

Making Gestures

Runes are quite physical to begin with; they have historically been carved into long lasting media like metals, leather, bone and horn, pottery, wood or bark and stone, rather than paper. The Norsemen also used physical gestures, like any people with spiritual beliefs, to protect themselves, invoke the Gods, to charge or consecrate magical items or attract good fortune. Whether they used the runes themselves in this way is not really known, but it is certainly another way in which a 21st century practitioner can use them for magic and protection.

The making of gestures is an intrinsic part of human behaviour, and one that the tide of atheism and spiritual apathy has not yet managed to eradicate. People still say, while performing the action, 'fingers crossed' or 'touch wood', and other gestures that had their origin in religious practice are still to be seen in everyday life, even though they may be accompanied by a self-conscious smirk. In modern magic we are quite accustomed to making magical signs in the air: witches' circles are created with gestures, and familiars and other spirits are summoned with them, deities are invoked and elementals welcomed or dismissed. Gestures are made to attract luck and happiness, and others to banish bad luck or negative spirits – what I like to call *beasties*. Whole spells, hexes too, can be cast using gestures only, by experienced practitioners. Many modern pagans – and probably ancient ones did too – use gestures as part of their private spiritual life, in prayers and as a prelude to meditating. Some will not approach their altars or working spaces without acknowledging the presence of the divine with gestures of respect and devotion.

Once you feel you have got to the heart of a rune, have marked its card and got its number, really understand as much about it as you can: you can move on to using the runes in a more physical way. Doing so involves having a deeper relationship with them than is necessary for simple divination or the creation of sigils; you must be ready to immerse yourself in the rune you are using, so that repetition of its name, for example, will become a magical mantra and not just a sound. This is not a symbol you have plucked from a book or website: it is a magical sign that speaks volumes to you (you may well find that some of the runes affect you this way – perhaps because they are tied in with a particular deity to whom you are drawn – while others do not). When, and only when you feel this way about any rune, are you ready to start working with it in a more physical way. The practice of using runes as gestures or bodily poses is called *Stadhagaldr*.

Runes as Gestures

Yeah, now we get to the bit I've been looking forward to with trepidation. Runes for the most part do not lend themselves to gestures using the hands, and you can end up with strained joints trying. And if you want to go one step further and use bindrunes in this way, well, you're on your own!

But... the use of the runes as hand gestures is potentially extremely valuable, an inconspicuous way of using the symbols in the office, the street or in a social situation, perhaps with your hands in your pockets for greater privacy, so it is well worthwhile trying to assimilate as many of the runic gestures as you can manage. Some of the runes do work quite well this way, and thankfully it is often the very useful ones that co-operate in this manner. Algiz, protection at your fingertips, can be shaped in the manner described in Chapter Two, or you could assume the position of the rune with your whole body (standing upright, feet together, arms stretched out in a Y shape) and pretend you are merely stretching. Jera, the rune of harvest and completion, can be formed with both hands facing and interlocking without actually touching, thumbs and forefingers spaced well apart. Isa can be formed with one finger, Gebo by crossing your two forefingers, Nauthiz by making the Christian 'fingers crossed' gesture and Fehu by flattening your thumb and smallest finger to your palm, turning your hand sideways, straightening out the forefinger and allowing the second and third fingers to space themselves below it (see what I mean… finger joint injury imminent!). If you're one of those people who can't rub their stomach and pat their head at the same time, forget it. Most of the others either take two hands or a lot of imagination, or both.

If you are reasonably good at visualisation, it is perhaps better to visualise the rune you want, perhaps emblazoned on your forehead for protection or on your hand for achievement. Or you might decide that the purely verbal use of the runes in the previous chapter is a much less complicated and more attractive idea.

Rune Walking

Meditation does not have to involve sitting on the floor in the lotus position with your hands posed in elaborate mudras on your knees. Children are taught to meditate while walking, as sitting still for active youngsters can prove a challenge. But walking is also an excellent way for an adult to connect with their inner self and with the runes. This can be done in the countryside, if you are fortunate enough to live near open fields and woodland, or in an urban park (it is not recommended to do it in a busy street with traffic passing). It can take several forms. Someone who is new to the runes might like to use the practice as a way of learning their order, meditating on each stave in turn as they walk, perhaps setting a time on the walk so that each rune is considered for a number of minutes before going on to the next one. Or the walk can focus on one rune at a time, or on the cast made that day, to try to draw all the meaning from it. Either way, the walker will return refreshed and almost certainly with more insights into the subject.

An open unstructured rune walk can simply allow the runes to appear in the mind, bringing their own messages, or perhaps appearing in physical ways in the scenery as you walk. Runes come from nature, and manifest easily in the shapes of trees and branches, hedgerow plants, clouds and airplane trails, bird formations and in many other ways. Try to look up, down and all around as you walk, to see them wherever they appear. If several runes appear, it is probably a good idea to jot them down in a notebook before you forget their order. However, this type of meditation needs a little discipline, or it can quickly deteriorate into thinking about the TV show you saw last night or what to make for dinner.

This exercise can also be used in situations where you are travelling by other means, for example on a train or in a car – preferably not when you are in the driver's seat!

Rune Dance

Many years ago, when I first started attending pagan moots, I saw a rune practitioner perform a rune dance, or *Galdrtanz*, in a crowded pub in Wiltshire. The sight very nearly reduced me to tears of laughter, and certainly amused the large number of muggles who were interested onlookers. Obviously, drink had been taken, but the fact that he was super serious about it simply made it even harder not to fall about laughing. The moral of this story is something to do with not casting your pearls before swine, but more about keeping your practices for an appropriate time and place, unless you want to end up as a meme on 4chan.

Since then, I have seen a number of versions of this dance, including posts on YouTube, which when performed like a ballet against a forest background or a sunset sea by a beautiful woman clad in flowing drapery, is much easier to take seriously, or perhaps I just grew up.

Full body gestures are much easier than hand gestures in depicting and evoking the runes, as the human body consists of an upright 'stave' with adjustable strokes attached. All but two of the runes, Hagalaz and Ingwaz, can be depicted this way (and the taller, later form of Ingwaz can also be depicted), even quite complex ones like Berkana and Mannaz. I have seen these poses described as 'runic yoga' and the hand gestures as 'runic mudras' (an interesting slant on Asian fusion). There is also a martial arts discipline based on the rune shapes. The poses are reasonably easy for anyone who has normal mobility, and even those with mobility challenges can assume some of the postures without too many problems. Some of them are performed seated, and it would probably not be beyond the wit of man to adapt most if not all of the poses for a seated person. Like any kind of exercise, they might very well improve the fitness and mobility of anyone who performed them regularly.

However, when you are at your altar or in a secluded outdoor spot where you plan to worship the Gods and do magic, you probably need include no more than one or two of the postures, though I would advise that you practise at home before a large mirror to make sure you can depict the rune recognisably.

The rune dance may take some time to master, as the full version involves knowing all the runes in order, and then learning how to form the shapes in a flowing dance, perhaps to music. But once it is learned, it becomes useful in many ways to any runemaster who is serious about their path. Performed as a moving meditation, it will attune the runemaster to the staves in a more spiritual way; just as Eastern yoga practices can bring about spiritual progress through physical actions.

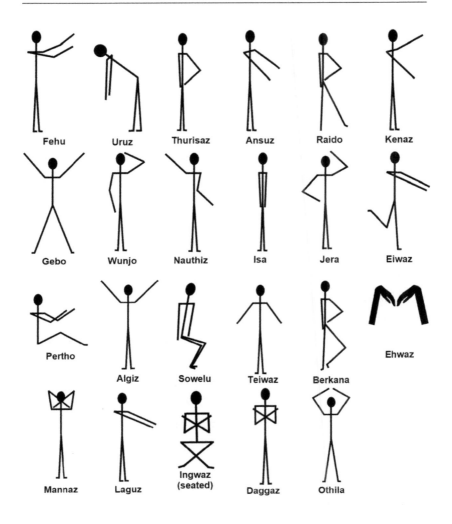

Fehu · Uruz · Thurisaz · Ansuz · Raido · Kenaz

Gebo · Wunjo · Nauthiz · Isa · Jera · Eiwaz

Pertho · Algiz · Sowelu · Teiwaz · Berkana · Ehwaz

Mannaz · Laguz · Ingwaz (seated) · Daggaz · Othila

Just like yoga, the exercises should be combined with controlled breathing and performed deliberately and slowly, especially when you are new to the discipline. Square breathing would be very suitable for this (this involves breathing in for a count of three or four, holding the breath for the same amount of time, breathing out for three or four, then pausing for the same time before inhaling again). Care should be taken not to strain either on the breath or the movements, which should be natural, unhurried and flowing.

The poses are performed slowly and gracefully, in the same manner as Tai Chi, each flowing into the next with little or no pause between them and, at the same time, the performer should make an effort to hold awareness, to feel the meaning and spirit of each rune as he or she adopts the appropriate pose. Thus, Fehu should evoke a feeling of contentedness and security, Kenaz should bring a feeling of heat and energy, Raido should bring a feeling of being in supreme control of the situation. The mind should be kept as still as possible during the dance, allowing the runes to flow through your entire being. Intuitions and messages will often result from this, and the mind is enabled to perceive truths that would perhaps not be accessible in other situations. The performer can call the name of each rune as it is performed, or a lengthened utterance of its sound.

The rune dance can also be used as an act of worship before your altar or in a private sacred space. Some carefully chosen slow music, perhaps pan pipes or harp, would be suitable for the mood of this dance. YouTube is stuffed with pagan and meditation music posts, and it wouldn't be difficult to find a piece of music that hits all your buttons and is the right tempo for the galdrtanz.

While the dance is excellent as a form of yogic exercise and can bring a deep sense of connection to the runes, as well as a feeling of physical wellbeing and relaxation, it can enhance magical work in other ways. The dance can be used as a type of spellwork in itself, or in support of other kinds of spellwork, dancing the postures for the chosen runes as part of the magical ritual, and perhaps returning to refresh the work that has been done by dancing and chanting at the same time each day. This is particularly effective with techniques such as crystal grids, which often need recharging every day with words and gestures to keep their power flowing for the required time.

The rune dance can also be enhanced by bringing tools and other items into the actions, such as using a wand in some of the gestures or holding selected crystals in the hands as the poses are performed. Runic symbols drawn on cards, flags or small wooden discs can also be carried in the hands, or even painted on the forehead or breast, or on the palms of the hands, to be revealed as part of the dance. Practitioners may decide to perform the dance skyclad (nude), which is a neopagan tradition of course, or they might wear special robes or other clothing kept specifically for magical work. Or they may decide to wear clothing in the *colour correspondences* of the rune(s) they are addressing; thus, light red for Fehu; dark blue for Ansuz; green for Berkana; and so on.

CHAPTER NINE

Signposts on the Pagan Path

Now we come to the last use of the runes and for many this will be the most important: as a source of spiritual progression. Many ancient spiritual practices were seen off in the ancient past by Christianity because they did not fit in with their world view. Christianity includes a transcendental view of deity; that is, the Christian God is seen as dwelling in the heavens, removed from, but overseeing human life from above. Modern pagans generally see deity as immanent, that is, involved in the physical world to such a degree that they comprise it; in Wicca we say, *we walk on the Goddess's body, we breathe Her breath*. These two rather different world views can be seen in the art of each spirituality: Christians depict their God as an elderly, fatherly man usually sitting in the clouds or sky, surrounded by angels, while pagan art usually depicts the Goddess as entwined in or made from natural matter or even pregnant with the Earth in her belly.

We are in process of rediscovering many of the ancient wisdoms our ancestors (of blood and of tradition) would have practised. Ancient pagans (and perhaps many of the modern ones) would have extended this belief in immanence to sacred sites, to rocks, stones, plants and other natural things, regarding them as having a spirit and even a consciousness of their own. This is called animism. They would have combined this with shamanism; the use of trance and other altered states of consciousness to contact and interact with the world of spirits and deity. Probably the most famous state of altered consciousness connected with the Norsemen is that of the berserker, the frenzied warrior... a state of mind in which the affected men fought heedless of wounds, and often without armour or shields, or even stark naked, carrying only their sword or axe. In this state, they were said to be almost invulnerable. The word berserker seems to mean *bear-shirt or bear-shirted*, which implies that they were possessed by their totem animals, or perhaps in some sense *became* the animal. The priesthoods of the ancient past would largely have been shamans, those whose path, training, and perhaps natural or hereditary abilities, equipped them with the capacity to intercede with the spirits and Gods on behalf of the tribe. Their training and subsequent practice would have included the use of hallucinogenic plants and fungi to induce trance and visions.

While you may not wish to join the old shaman's banquet of moulds, toadstools and slightly poisonous plants, bringing the runes into your life will almost certainly cause them to take you into theirs: they will lead you on further paths, down the rabbit hole, through the wardrobe door and into other worlds. My advice is: let them. You will be the richer for it.

Meditation

I have written earlier in this book about the importance of meditating with each rune as you get to know it, but maintaining your relationship is also very important, especially if you intend to use the staves for magic. If you are reading this book, odds-on you are already pretty familiar with spiritual practices such as meditation, but I will give a few pointers. Let's start with the three P's.

Privacy: this is a no-brainer, I admit, but vital. The number of times I have been roughly roused from meditation by the telephone, the doorbell, coffee-proffering husband, clean shirt-seeking son or nagging cat may well take some of the blame for the fact that I am an indifferent and, I am afraid, also an infrequent meditator. Constant interruptions like this, or those caused internally by Monkey Mind and one's own natural inability to sit still and get on with the damn job do unfortunately damage your ability to meditate. Some effects can be mitigated: take the landline receiver off the hook and mute your mobile. Take the batteries out of the doorbell if you think you can get away with it. Threaten family members with dire consequences (nothing you can do about the cat) and hang a sign on the room door saying that you are meditating and must not be disturbed.

Posture: the lotus position is all very well for Eastern mystics and experienced yoga practitioners, but don't tie yourself in knots just because you have an illustration of some limber yogi doing it on a CD cover somewhere. Comfort, or more accurately absence of discomfort, is more important and indeed vital to the practice of meditation. Sit cross-legged if you find it easy. It is possible to buy tiny meditation stools and firm foam blocks for use in this position if, like me, you find yourself tipping backwards when you try it. This aligns the spine to the vertical, which is a much more easily maintainable posture, and keeps your chakras in a straight line as well. If this position is not for you, treat your creaking joints to the comfort of a chair, either a hard kitchen-type chair or a fairly upright armchair. Too much comfort may cause you to fall asleep, so it is necessary to strike a happy medium. The room should be warm, but not so warm that you may nod off. Sit with your legs uncrossed, feet flat to the floor and your hands laid loosely in your lap. I do not recommend lying down. The important thing is to strike a balance between being uncomfortable and being so comfortable that you become sleepy.

Peripherals: ambience can be as important as physical comfort (or lack of discomfort anyway) in aiding concentration in spiritual practice. Experienced practitioners will recognise what I am talking about when I say the conditions created by certain types of lighting, certain music, certain fragrances, can take you halfway there before you begin. Harp music or Tibetan singing bowls are particularly good for this. If you have a selection of these tracks on your phone, you can achieve a fairly meditative state anywhere, e.g. airport lounges, parks, in the office or on the bus. And, of course, listening to your meditation music through earbuds will make it harder for outside sounds to disturb your practice. If you have a space that you use for magic or worship, this is probably the space you should use for meditation, and the room should be equipped with whatever helps you achieve the right frame of mind.

I personally find a short prayer to one's patron deity is helpful before you begin. Some nice deep breaths, or square breathing, are the next step, while you gradually allow your shoulders to peel down from over your ears and other parts of your body to relax as fully as you are able — deliberately pushing your belly out as you breathe is another useful technique. Most people unconsciously hold in their stomachs to some degree and few of us breathe as deeply down into our bellies as we should.

The mind is then cleared of all thoughts and distractions and allowed to go its own way in peace, perhaps using a mantra. Here is where the rune names come into their own. If you are travelling with a single rune, its name can be your mantra: there are examples of this kind of chanting to be found online, and with the appropriate music it can be very effective. A mantra is a very good way of stilling Monkey Mind, by choking its chatter with another sound or thought. Or concentrating on the breath is another good way of achieving the change in brainwave rhythms and, if the mind wanders (as it will), it can be gently returned to the breath again.

I find taking one particular point of the experience of breathing is helpful. For example, the sensation of the air entering your nostrils or the slow rhythmic movement of the diaphragm as it draws in and pushes out the air. Focus on this to the exclusion of all other sensations.

This is the essence of meditation, a calm state in which the mind is stilled, and thoughts are gently pushed away, but we are discussing runes here, and how they can fit into this practice. As the mind becomes still, it is time to focus on the subject you have chosen for the meditation, whether this is one rune or whether you are meditating on the runes themselves in all their mystery and magic, or whether it is a God or Goddess from the Norse pantheon.

Have the rune you have chosen before your mental eyes. If you find this difficult, imagine yourself in a cinema and, as the curtains open, see the rune emblazoned on the screen before you (this idea can be expanded to include preparation, by visualising yourself walking up steps into the cinema, then walking along aisles until you find your seat). Experienced meditators have usually developed all kinds of tricks like this to help them in their practice. Do nothing else actively: allow the rune to tell you what it will. Use it as a sort of visual mantra, to prevent your mind from wandering back to everyday thoughts and worries, and you may be surprised at what comes to you. Watch it on the screen – does it change size or colour? Does it emit a sound, or perhaps music? With a little adjustment, this technique can be used for more than one rune, or for the entire set. The secret is utter openness and relaxation, with no attempt to force the mind in a particular direction; in fact, this can lead to strain and you may come out of the meditation with a headache. Don't worry if you find it difficult at first: it will take practice. We are so accustomed, especially in the 21st century, to being in control, to having everything at our fingertips and a remote in our hand, that letting go in this way does not come very naturally.

Do not forget that meditation does not need to be done sitting; as I mentioned earlier, it can be performed while walking in a safe environment, or while performing routine tasks that require no attention, such as peeling potatoes, washing up, hoovering the carpet, mowing the lawn, washing the car. With some people, the mind enters a meditative state while driving a car, but I do not recommend this.

If you are new to meditation, try for ten minutes or so the first time, and gradually increase this until you are meditating for 40 minutes or so. The practice is ideally used at least once every day, but you may find considerable resistance to this from your own will and from life itself. Do what you can; it will get better, and it will bring many benefits in the form of a better ability to deal with stress and even improved health, for example lowered blood pressure, and can improve other conditions that are exacerbated by stress, such as IBS.

Don't worry either that the meditation will become so deep that you will never awaken from it: you should be so lucky! The meditation will last as long as it needs to, then you will gently awaken, but just as likely is that someone or something from the outside world will gain your attention.

Many people consider meditation to be impossible because they 'never have time', but everyone has some free time. Even if it's just a few minutes, it will make a difference. Try setting your alarm for a few minutes earlier in the morning or taking a few minutes before you go to bed. Meditate in the bath! Once the habit is established, you will find it easier and you will reap benefits both physically and spiritually; meditation can also mitigate insomnia and aid restful sleep.

Pathworking

Daily meditation as described above is quite a passive activity, but the same basic practices can be used for a more proactive form called pathworking, which is the beginnings of shamanism. Pathworking can be used for gaining insights, meeting spirits, totem animals and guides and learning not only about our inner selves but about ancient wisdoms such as the runes. There is a simply immense variety of ways in which this practice can be used, from contemplating and communing with a single symbol to the Hawaiian rite called Ho'oponopono, which conjures a person you no longer see, from whom you are estranged or even a person no longer alive, so you can reconcile an old difference with them.

Just as with meditation, you must relax the body and still the mind, and breathing exercises such as square breathing are excellent for this. I would recommend that you do a full body relaxation, which involves starting either at the crown of the head or the toes and relaxing each part of you, toe by toe, finger by finger, until you reach the other end of the body. In a group, this is usually done by a delegated member gently murmuring instructions, but you could also use a recording. Quiet music, or other sound effects – try whale song, for example – can be played and incense burned, until you have achieved the calm receptive state needed.

The most important thing with pathworkings is to have no agenda, no preconceptions, to just *be* in the practice and allow experiences to come to you. What validity would the experience have if you took the wheel and controlled what you saw? That's just daydreaming.

Pathworking can be done in a group, with one member reading the journey slowly, while the other group members experience it by visualisation. This is how I was first introduced to the runes in depth myself, and it certainly did the trick. But if you do not have access to a group of like-minded people, the best way of kicking off your individual practice is by using a recording of what you will experience.

If you have a script you have written yourself, record it, speaking slowly, to use in the session. Always leave plenty of opportunity and pauses in the script for the pathworking to go its own way: do not, for example, decide what entities encountered in the journey will say, or what they will do – leave this to unfold naturally.

Start with a quite simple scenario: perhaps wander around a garden seeing magical plants and meeting animals or people, or you can sail across a magical lake or ocean, or even fly. Do not, at this stage, attempt anything that is likely to be upsetting or frightening – and these experiences can be, even though they are 'all in the mind'. Sometimes creatures in the scene will speak to you or give you gifts: these are messages that should be remembered for when you come out of the pathworking. I once had a beautiful green crystal given me by a Goddess figure while I was taking part in a group pathworking at a psychic fair. Minutes later, I found the self-same crystal, at a knockdown price, on a stall right outside the door. Did I buy it? Too right! It is still an important part of my individual practice.

Here is an example of a simple pathworking I wrote to include in a coven ritual to connect with Odin. It is quite long, but could be useful as a means of trying out the techniques I have mentioned. Record the text on your phone or other device, speaking very slowly and allowing plenty of pauses where indicated for the action of the narrative. If you can't stand the sound of your own voice (and I know that feeling!) ask someone else to record it for you. Then you can use the recording as you enter the meditative state (and even utilise the pause button if the recording goes too fast for you):

Odin is the God who breathed His breath into the first human beings, imbuing them with life. He is the breath-giver, and our continued breath is His gift. The first breath we take is drawn from Him and the last breath we exhale will be given back to Him. That is the focus of this meditation, that primal connection, that spiritual umbilicus.

Sitting comfortably, begin to focus on your breath. Feel the coolness of the breath as you inhale. Allow yourself to feel the intercostals (the muscles between your ribs) expand and release. Spend a few moments focusing on the inhalation, the feel of the breath flowing into your lungs, the expansion of your diaphragm followed by the exhalation, the rush of breath leaving your lungs, the contraction. Become aware of the circular rhythm and once you have spent a few moments focusing on your breath, turn your attention to Odin.

As you breathe, think about the creation story. Think about that first kiss of breath, the moment that Odin breathed life into the first man and woman, Askr and Embla, waking them to their own humanity. Think about what that set in motion, and the long progression of humanity that flowed from the moment of that kiss.

Visualize, feel, or imagine that you are connected to Odin by the cord of your breath, by that very rhythm of the inhalation and exhalation of your breathing. Imagine that as you inhale, you are consciously drinking in His breath, that He is breathing into you, and as you exhale, you are breathing into Him and He is drinking in your breath.

PAUSE.

Now you stand before His throne in Asgard, this most radiant palace made from gold and precious stones, and lit with eternal sunlight. Odin sits in splendour, yet He does not cause you any fear as He turns His one eye on you, an eye as blue as a summer sky... there is something about Him that reminds you subtly of an older man you knew and loved as a child, perhaps your grandfather. His hair and beard are long and grey, and He is dressed in homely garments which do not seem in keeping with the splendour in which you find Him.

He rises from His throne and steps towards you, taking your hand just as though you are a child. On the instant that His hand touches yours, Asgard melts away, and you find yourself alone with Him on a remote winding highway that runs between high mountains. Dusk is falling, and against the red-streaked sky can be seen the outlines of rather scrubby trees along the path. You stand surprised, and Odin smiles at you. Now He wears a rather dusty cloak of dark blue, a broad-brimmed traveller's hat, scuffed and with a broken brim, and carries a traveller's staff cut from a hedge. His ravens Huginn and Muninn sit on His shoulders, and at a distance two wolves are running around sniffing and exploring like dogs, free but never wandering too far from Him.

'Where are we going?' you ask Him, but He only shakes His head and walks on, muttering to His wolves and ravens.

The path is hard and stony, but when you stumble, His hand tightens on yours to prevent you from falling, and He never walks so fast that you cannot keep up.

The dusk deepens and one star comes out. The path is long and you are tired, yet Odin walks on giving no sign of weariness. Slowly the Moon rises on your left, and you see that She is glinting on the distant sea. It starts to become very cold, and soon rime is glittering on Odin's shoulders and every breath you take comes out as a thick white fog.

You stumble at last, and beg Him to slow down. He stops, turns, sees you shivering, and suddenly you are clad in a thick warm cloak with a fur-lined hood, and are warm as toast. From nowhere, He produces a great silver-mounted horn and hands it to you. It is so large you can almost not hold it, but you drink from it... delicious warm mead, and suddenly you are filled with renewed strength.

'Not far now,' He says, then chuckles. 'And yet very far... how far is it to the centre of a pebble? Yet no man has been there.'

This strange thought keeps you thinking as you journey on with Him, and before you have noticed anything before you, you find you and He are entering a great cave mouth half hidden by bushes and hanging ivy. Despite the cloak, you begin to be chilled again, this time with fear, but Odin draws you on, chuckling a little at your reluctance.

The floor of the cave leads inwards and then slopes gently down. It is pitch dark, so you rely on Odin's hand to lead you without stumbling. His ravens croak ominously in the dark and the wolves whine and grumble, but you swallow your fear and follow on.

After what seems a very long journey down into the earth, the air becomes warmer and there is at last some light, a reddish glow ahead. Suddenly you turn a corner in the tunnel and find a blazing fire and three hooded figures sitting around it. A cauldron hangs over the fire, giving off a bitter aroma of herbs.

Odin greets the figures like old friends.

They stand, and the foremost throws off Her hood, revealing an ancient lady with bright eyes and long moon-white hair. She greets Odin, and the second also drops Her hood, revealing a beautiful mature lady with golden tresses elaborately plaited and bound on Her head. The third does not stand, nor does She take off Her hood, but sits silently by the cauldron. All that can be seen of Her is a slim, young hand which reaches out to stir the brew from time to time.

Suddenly the Sisters are standing around you, looking at you, even the Veiled One, with curiosity.

'What would you see?' asks old Urd.

Odin speaks for you. 'My passion,' He says.

Verdandi, the lady with golden hair, takes you by the hand and leads you to a corner where huge ancient roots bulge from the cave wall. Here among the roots is a deep hole, rimmed around with ferns and crystals and, as you lean over, you can see below you the dark glimmer of water. As you watch, you see your immortal guide hanging, naked and wounded, over the well, blood dripping from His self-inflicted wound, His face contorted with agony. Horrified, you draw back from the vision.

'Look!' cries hooded Skuld in Her young girl's voice, and again you look down into the black water that lies like a scrying mirror below you.

What do you see? For this is your future path… what will you learn? What sacrifices will you make to gain the wisdom you seek?

PAUSE

The vision fades. You turn from the well and find Skuld waiting for you, Her dark hood pulled away and Her beautiful young face revealed. Is She glad or sorry? Angry or pleased? Does She have a message for you?

PAUSE

Kneel before the Nornir now and thank Them each for Their help. If you *wish, ask Them to be in your life and a part of your path, for They are the keepers of all wisdom.*

It is time to go. Odin is saying farewell to the Sisters, and now He takes your hand and leads you away, back down the long dark tunnel and away from the cheery fire. The journey is long, but soon you are out of the cave and standing upon the lonely road across the moor, the Moon shining full upon you both.

'Farewell my child,' says Odin, and you thank Him for His guidance and take your leave of Him.

Return.

Do not be limited to pathworkings you find in books or online: remember; the pathworking is only a framework. This one is quite detailed, but a pathworking need not be. You can start a journey anywhere, with no more information than that you are standing on a beach or in a deep forest, and let it take you where it will. These kinds of journeys are often the most rewarding, as they are completely free and open to anything that comes up, and they do not require a recording (you can maybe play some meditation music very quietly if you need this). Each rune can be taken with you as you work, perhaps as a wand or staff that you carry in your hand as you journey. Take a little time as you enter the pathworking to build your rune accessory: is it a staff or a wand, or a pendant around your neck? Feel its weight, feel the rough or smooth wood or other material of the artefact. Really create it, before you begin, then it will be easier to keep it with you through the journey.

Rune Initiation

At some point on their way, serious practitioners may well feel the need of an initiation or other marking of their commitment to working with the runes. While there are organisations and individuals online who will offer initiation, this is usually expensive and probably not tailored for the individual rune practitioner. When it comes to initiation, one size does not fit all.

My own preference, for any practice that does not involve a longstanding and still extant initiatory tradition, would be informed self-initiation. The old runemasters died centuries ago, taking much of their wisdom with them, and all that remains is modern people who, whatever their degree of skill and knowledge, have access to no better than the same sources from which you are acquiring your own skills.

When you are ready for this step, take some time and thought before you start designing your own ritual. What will you include? Which deities will you invoke? What vows will you write and speak? When will you perform the ritual? This latter is also important, as many people feel a rite carried out on an auspicious date is more meaningful than one done on the spur of the moment. Choose a date that is special to you, or choose a pagan Sabbat, or an astrological event such as a Full or New Moon.

The content of initiations usually takes a fairly regular course: some form of purification by way of preparation and, in some cases, some form of ordeal to prove the candidate is worthy, followed by the swearing of oaths and some actions symbolising the entry to the new path. These could include symbols written on the body in oil, charged water or even blood, the putting on of ritual clothing or jewellery, such as a ritual pendant, or a belt inscribed with magical characters. The ritual usually continues with an enactment to prove the initiate knows their magical onions, and some kind of presentation of the successful candidate, to the Gods or to those assembled. Finally, there is a communion-style drinking or sharing of wine, and maybe also the eating of some special food, both substances having been blessed earlier in the rite. This of course would be an initiation carried out by a master to initiate a protégé, but with a little thought it would be easy to adapt this outline for one person to initiate themself.

A suggested self-initiation might take the following outline form, but you can personalize it or add whatever components seem good to you:

- Start with prayer and meditation to prepare oneself, and certainly a ritual bath or shower, and the putting on of any ritual clothing normally worn for rune magic or practice.
- The altar would be set up as for normal ritual, with candles and incense, and include the runes, perhaps laid out in a circle in the centre, in their right order. There would be an appropriate drink, perhaps mead, and a little bread or cake. There is a reason we eat and drink after a ritual: it grounds the body and the mind after an event that can be exciting and can leave the person 'wired' so they cannot settle or sleep afterwards: most witches have experienced this kind of reaction. Any other runic tools can be laid out on the altar, if there is space, and a bell should be included, also any images of deities you honour: Odin is a pretty obvious choice here, or the Norns, but if you are not otherwise drawn to Norse traditions, choose a God or Goddess of wisdom such as Isis, Athene, Thoth, Ogma or Mercury. You could include a candle for each deity you invoke, or even 24 candles, one for each of the runes. In some traditions it is appropriate to include items representing the four elements: a candle for fire, a bowl of water, a stone or bowl of soil for earth and a censer, feather, scented flower or bell for air. You can also dress the altar with any flowers, herbs or crystals you feel are appropriate.
- Smudging the space you plan to use is another good idea. Almost all magic shops sell smudging wands of dried sage, or you could easily make your own if you have sage in the garden. The bundle is lit at one end and the flame gently blown out so it smoulders, and the aromatic smoke is wafted around the space: you will be amazed at the difference this makes to the general feeling of the room, and for quite some time

afterwards. Suitable incense can be lit: some magic shops will actually have 'initiation' incense labelled as such, or again, you can make your own.

- All this should have had an effect on your mind and spirit; you may well feel strangely calm and at the same time a little excited. This is the mindset you are looking for. A Wiccan, and some other magical practitioners, might now cast a circle, invoke the Element Lords and also their Gods before they begin. This is up to you, but if casting up is not something you are accustomed to doing, it might feel wrong and inappropriate, and even spoil the sense of occasion you have acquired. If you do wish to cast a circle, it might be appropriate to Norse it up, invoking for the element wards the spirits of Alfheim for air, Muspellheim for fire, Vanaheim or Niflheim for water and Svartalfheim for earth. You can have an item that represents each element laid at the corresponding quarters (and this can be on your altar or in the four corners of the room), such as a feather, candle, bowl of water and stone, or you could get more runic and lay appropriate runes in the quarters: perhaps Ansuz for air, Kenaz for fire, Laguz for water and Jera for earth.

- Sit at your altar and light the candles and incense. Bless the wine and food you are using, with any words and gestures that you might normally use. When you are ready, ring the bell softly. This signals to the Gods (and to yourself) that you are ready to begin.

- Chant, sing or speak the rune names from Fehu to Othila, perhaps touching each one as you name it and lighting its candle, if you have set out candles for the runes themselves. Speak to the runes; tell them all they mean to you, and perhaps speak vows to them and to the invoked deities about your future path with them. When this is complete, stay quiet for a few minutes, empty your mind and wait to see if any messages come to you.

- If you have dedicated a piece of jewellery or a belt or other regalia, bless it and offer it to the Gods and the runes, then put it on.
- Offer wine and whatever food you have, and eat and drink yourself.
- Put out the candles. Close the circle, if you cast one, and go away from the area where you have been working, returning later to clean and tidy respectfully.

Self-initiation can seem a little inadequate, though often of course it is the only option available. If you belong to a runic group, or other magical group, you may stage your initiation with like-minded friends, and make a party of it, perhaps with others who would like to be initiated. If someone in the group has any kind of seniority or expertise, they can perhaps act as High Priest and conduct the ritual, which could still follow the same rough outline as the suggestions given above.

Then there is the possibility that you belong to, or even lead, a runic magic community online, and that you and the members of your group can come together by group video chat or on a conferencing platform to enact the ritual. Hmm, I hear you saying, *ritual online?* How does that work? I can assure you that it does. During the Covid lockdown, two of my initiates were prepared for their Wiccan Second Degree initiations, and were in for a long wait for their deserved and eagerly awaited rituals. One of them lived abroad, with no prospect of getting to the UK in the foreseeable future for the initiation to be done face to face. In the end we decided to give online ritual a try, and each attendee prepared their own sacred space, with the one addition of an IT device such as a tablet or laptop. Scripts were sent beforehand, and where one attendee needed a substance, such as a particular anointing oil, or other piece of kit, this was posted to them. In both cases, the initiates reported that they felt properly 'churched', that the rite was sacred and meaningful, and they were glad they had agreed to do it. However, many people would not be comfortable performing skyclad ritual by these means as there are too many stories of these apps being hacked or sessions invaded by outsiders.

The Cycle of Initiation of 13 Runes

This is a 21st century construct based on the idea of working with a series of runes that will lead you, through meditations and other exercises, to a more developed spirituality. The runes were supposedly chosen for their abilities to change the inner self. There are a few of these more modern ideas about, which are based on the work of contemporary runemasters, for example rune dances.

The runes in this sequence are: Ansuz (signals, messages), Othila (separation and retreat), Uruz (strength), Pertho (mystery and initiation), Nauthiz (pain and necessity), Ingwaz (new beginnings), Kenaz (knowledge, insight), Berkana (rebirth), Ehwaz (progress), Hagalaz (disruption), Raido (the journey), Thurisaz (gateway) and Daggaz (breakthrough, enlightenment). The cycle is undertaken by meditating upon each rune in turn until the final rune is reached, when a powerful cumulative message is received. This exercise should be undertaken with a due commitment of time: don't imagine you can 'do' all the runes in an afternoon and magically become a runemaster! It would be advisable to start the journey on a meaningful date, as is often advised for any magical work, and give each rune at least a day to itself, and probably much longer. Often, the runes will take their own time and may give you their messages within half an hour...or take a month. It is important not to hurry this process... what, you've got something better to do? If it is important to you, you will understand that the time is an offering in itself, and part of the respect you should give the runes. If you don't respect them, how will you expect them to work with you?

You may feel that this idea is superfluous, and that your own journey with the runes has already got this covered. My feeling is that the runes are in an agreed order for a reason; they were once part of an oral tradition, and the order in which they were set down is the order in which they should be used.

One last word on runic shamanism. Although the taking of substances like mescaline, psilocybin and ayahuasca have become part of the spiritual path of some witches and pagans, I would not recommend taking any kind of drug to aid you willy-nilly in meditation or pathworking. However, the British wayside plant mugwort (*Artemisia vulgaris*), an easily identified species related to wormwood, is helpful in a simple tisane before working: 2tbs of the chopped herb in a pint of boiling water, left to stand and then strained. It is foully bitter, so a teaspoon of honey may be needed. This should not be taken too often, however, and care must be taken to identify the plant properly. Although easy to see in grassy verges with its silvery feathery leaves, mugwort is a late plant and will not be large enough to see much before June, flowering around August to September. It dries well and can then be chopped up and stored in a jar. I do not recommend buying its essential oil, as this may include other ingredients. Mugwort is one of the Nine Sacred Herbs of Odin, which are listed in Chapter Five.

The Rune Poems

I have included all three poems for interest. The 8th/9th century Anglo-Saxon rune poem is especially fascinating, as it is possible to see the roots of the English language there, with many words almost as we know them today. Bear in mind that the poems were extensively edited by Christian clergy, who replaced pagan references with Christian ones, especially in the AS version.

The Anglo-Saxon poem is the only one that includes all 24 letters equivalent to the runes in the Futhark alphabet; in later alphabets letters had been changed or omitted as the languages developed and pronunciation changed. In fact, the AS rune poem has five additional letters (not included), which are irrelevant to our subject, as five additional vowels had been added. This alphabet is called the Futhorc.

There is sadly no rune poem actually written for the Elder Futhark, or none that has survived, yet the AS poem includes all the relevant letters, though they may have different names, and keeps to the original order as well. The 13th century Norwegian and 15th century Icelandic rune poems have only 16 verses but, where a verse has been given to a letter that is equivalent to a Futhark rune, it can still be studied for meaning.

In each case, I have used the Futhark rune names to identify each verse, to avoid confusion, and rearranged the verses into the Futhark order.

The poems are rich in 'kennings', the little word games the Norsemen loved to play with names. You will see 'fishes' bath' as a name for the sea, and 'sea steed' for a boat. Gods may be identified by a kenning, with Odin having the lion's share of these, based on his adventures. It is important to look out for these, as not only is it harder to understand the verse without appreciating that part of it may be a kenning, but often there are messages hidden within the kennings themselves. For example, in the Norwegian poem the verse concerning Ansuz reads, *'Rivermouth begins the journey, yet the scabbard is for the sword.'* Rather than taking the words at their face value, go deeper: does this speak of the wisdom of watching what you say, of avoiding a quarrel and the resulting violence? Is Rivermouth a kenning for someone who cannot keep their mouth shut?

The Anglo-Saxon Rune Poem (Old English)

FEHU: Feoh byþ frofur fira gehwylcum;
            sceal ðeah manna gehwylc miclun hyt dælan
            gif he wile for drihtne domes hleotan.

URUZ: Ur byþ anmod ond oferhyrned,
            felafrecne deor, feohteþ mid hornum mære
            morstapa; þæt is modig wuht.

THURISAZ: Ðorn byþ ðearle scearp; ðegna gehwylcum
            anfeng ys yfyl, ungemetum reþe
            manna gehwelcum, ðe him mid resteð.

ANSUZ: Os byþ ordfruma ælere spræce,
            wisdomes wraþu ond witena frofur
            and eorla gehwam eadnys ond tohiht.

RAIDO: Rad byþ on recyde rinca gehwylcum
            sefte ond swiþhwæt, ðamðe sitteþ on ufan
            meare mægenheardum ofer milpaþas.

KENAZ: Cen byþ cwicera gehwam, cuþ on fyre
            blac ond beorhtlic, byrneþ oftust
            ðær hi æþelingas inne restaþ.

GEBO: Gyfu gumena byþ gleng and herenys,
wraþu and wyrþscype and wræcna gehwam
ar and ætwist, ðe byþ oþra leas.

WUNJO: Wenne bruceþ, ðe can weana lyt
sares and sorge and him sylfa hæfþ
blæd and blysse and eac byrga geniht.

HAGALAZ: Hægl byþ hwitust corna; hwyrft hit of heofones lyfte,
wealcaþ hit windes scura; weorþeþ hit to wætere
syððan.

NAUTHIZ: Nyd byþ nearu on breostan; weorþeþ hi þeah oft niþa
bearnum to helpe and to hæle gehwæþre, gif hi his
hlystaþ æror.

ISA: Is byþ ofereald, ungemetum slidor,
glisnaþ glæshluttur gimmum gelicust,
flor forste geworuht, fæger ansyne.

JERA: Ger byÞ gumena hiht, ðonne God læteþ,
halig heofones cyning, hrusan syllan
beorhte bleda beornum ond ðearfum.

EIWAZ: Eoh byþ utan unsmeþe treow,
heard hrusan fæst, hyrde fyres,
wyrtrumun underwreþyd, wyn on eþle.

PERTHO: Peorð byþ symble plega and hlehter
wlancum [on middum], ðar wigan sittaþ
on beorsele bliþe ætsomne.

ALGIZ: Eolh-secg eard hæfþ oftust on fenne
wexeð on wature, wundaþ grimme,
blode breneð beorna gehwylcne
ðe him ænigne onfeng gedeþ.

SOWELU: Sigel semannum symble biþ on hihte,
ðonne hi hine feriaþ ofer fisces beþ,
oþ hi brimhengest bringeþ to lande.

TEIWAZ: Tir biþ tacna sum, healdeð trywa wel
wiþ æþelingas; a biþ on færylde

ofer nihta genipu, næfre swiceþ.

BERKANA: Beorc byþ bleda leas, bereþ efne swa ðeah
tanas butan tudder, biþ on telgum wlitig,
heah on helme hrysted fægere,
geloden leafum, lyfte getenge.

EHWAZ: Eh byþ for eorlum æþelinga wyn,
hors hofum wlanc, ðær him hæleþ ymb[e]
welege on wicgum wrixlaþ spræce
and biþ unstyllum æfre frofur.

MANNAZ: Man byþ on myrgþe his magan leof:
sceal þeah anra gehwylc oðrum swican,
forðum drihten wyle dome sine
þæt earme flæsc eorþan betæcan.

LAGUZ: Lagu byþ leodum langsum geþuht,
gif hi sculun neþan on nacan tealtum
and hi sæyþa swyþe bregaþ
and se brimhengest bridles ne gym[eð].

INGWAZ: Ing wæs ærest mid East-Denum
gesewen secgun, oþ he siððan est
ofer wæg gewat; wæn æfter ran;
ðus Heardingas ðone hæle nemdun.

OTHILA: Eþel byþ oferleof æghwylcum men,
gif he mot ðær rihtes and gerysena on
brucan on bolde bleadum oftast.

DAGGAZ: Dæg byþ drihtnes sond, deore mannum,
mære metodes leoht, myrgþ and tohiht
eadgum and earmum, eallum brice.

The Anglo-Saxon Rune Poem (Translation)

FEHU: Wealth is a comfort to all men,
yet must every man bestow it freely,
if he would gain honour in the sight of the Lord.

URUZ: The aurochs is proud and has great horns;
it is a very savage beast and fights with its horns;
a great ranger of the moors, it is a creature of mettle.

THURISAZ: The thorn is exceedingly sharp,
an evil thing for any knight to touch,
uncommonly severe on all who sit among them.

ANSUZ: The mouth is the source of all language,
a pillar of wisdom and a comfort to wise men,
a blessing and a joy to every knight.

RAIDO: Riding seems easy to every warrior while he is
indoors and very courageous to him who traverses
the high roads
on the back of a stout horse.

KENAZ: The torch is known to every living man by its pale,
bright flame; it always burns where princes sit
within.

GEBO: Generosity brings credit and honour, which support
one's dignity; it furnishes help and subsistence to all
broken men who are devoid of aught else.

WUNJO: Bliss he enjoys who knows not suffering, sorrow nor
anxiety, and has prosperity and happiness and a good
enough house.

HAGALAZ: Hail is the whitest of grain;
it is whirled from the vault of heaven
and is tossed about by gusts of wind
and then it melts into water.

NAUTHIZ: Trouble is oppressive to the heart; yet often it proves
a source of help and salvation to the children of men,
to everyone who heeds it betimes.

ISA: Ice is very cold and immeasurably slippery;
it glistens as clear as glass and most like to gems;
it is a floor wrought by the frost, fair to look upon.

JERA: Summer is a joy to men, when God, the holy King of
Heaven, suffers the earth to bring forth shining fruits
for rich and poor alike.

EIWAZ: The yew is a tree with rough bark,
hard and fast in the earth, supported by its roots,
a guardian of flame and a joy upon an estate.

PERTHO: *Peorth* is a source of recreation and amusement to
the great, where warriors sit merrily together in the
banqueting-hall.

ALGIZ: The elk-sedge is mostly to be found in a marsh;
it grows in the water and makes a ghastly wound,
covering with blood every warrior who touches it.

SOWELU: The Sun is ever a joy in the hopes of seafarers
when they journey away over the fishes' bath,
until the sea steed deep bears them to land.

TEIWAZ: Tiw is a guiding star; well does it keep faith with
princes; it is ever on its course over the mists of
night and never fails.

BERKANA: The birch bears no fruit; yet without seed it brings
forth suckers, for it is generated from its leaves.
Splendid are its branches and gloriously adorned its
lofty crown which reaches to the skies.

EHWAZ: The horse is a joy to princes in the presence of
warriors. A steed in the pride of its hoofs,
when rich men on horseback bandy words about
it; and it is ever a source of comfort to the restless.

MANNAZ: The joyous man is dear to his kinsmen;
yet every man is doomed to fail his fellow,
since the Lord by his decree will commit the
wretched flesh to the earth.

LAGUZ: The ocean seems interminable to men,
if they venture on the rolling bark
and the waves of the sea terrify them
and the sea steed heeds not its bridle.

INGWAZ: Ing was first seen by men among the East-Danes,
till, followed by his chariot,
he departed eastwards over the waves.
So the Heardingas named the hero.

OTHILA: An estate is very dear to every man,
if he can enjoy there in his house
whatever is right and proper in constant prosperity.

DAGGAZ: Day, the glorious light of the Creator, is sent by the
Lord; it is beloved of men, a source of hope and
happiness to rich and poor, and of service to all.

The Icelandic Rune Poem (Old Icelandic)

FEHU: Fé er frænda róg
ok flæðar viti
ok grafseiðs gata
aurum fylkir.

URUZ: Úr er skýja grátr
ok skára þverrir
ok hirðis hatr.
umbre vísi

THURISAZ: Þurs er kvenna kvöl
ok kletta búi
ok varðrúnar verr.
Saturnus þengill.

ANSUZ: Óss er algingautr
ok ásgarðs jöfurr,
ok valhallar vísi.
Jupiter oddviti.

RAIDO: Reið er sitjandi sæla

ok snúðig ferð
ok jórs erfiði.
iter ræsir.

KENAZ: Kaun er barna böl
ok bardaga [för]
ok holdfúa hús.
flagella konungr.

HAGALAZ: Hagall er kaldakorn
ok krapadrífa
ok snáka sótt.
grando hildingr.

NAUTHIZ: Nauð er Þýjar þrá
ok þungr kostr
ok vássamlig verk.
opera niflungr.

ISA: Íss er árbörkr
ok unnar þak
ok feigra manna fár.
glacies jöfurr.

JERA: Ár er gumna góði
ok gott sumar
algróinn akr.
annus allvaldr.

EIWAZ: Ýr er bendr bogi
ok brotgjarnt járn
ok fífu fárbauti.
arcus ynglingr.

SOWELU: Sól er skýja skjöldr
ok skínandi röðull
ok ísa aldrtregi.
rota siklingr.

TEIWAZ: Týr er einhendr áss
ok ulfs leifar

ok hofa hilmir.
Mars tiggi.

BERKANA: Bjarkan er laufgat lim
ok lítit tré
ok ungsamligr viðr.
abies buðlungr.

MANNAZ: Maðr er manns gaman
ok moldar auki
ok skipa skreytir.
homo mildingr.

LAGUZ: Lögr er vellanda vatn
ok viðr ketill
ok glömmungr grund.
lacus lofðungr.

The Icelandic Rune Poem (Translation)

FEHU: Wealth
source of discord among kinsmen
and fire of the sea
and path of the serpent.

URUZ: Shower
lamentation of the clouds
and ruin of the hay-harvest
and abomination of the shepherd.

THURISAZ: Giant
torture of women
and cliff-dweller
and husband of a giantess.

ANSUZ: God
aged Gautr
and prince of Ásgarðr
and Lord of Vallhalla.

RAIDO: Riding

joy of the horsemen
and speedy journey
and toil of the steed.

KENAZ: Ulcer
disease fatal to children
and painful spot
and abode of mortification.

HAGALAZ: Hail
cold grain
and shower of sleet
and sickness of serpents.

NAUTHIZ: Constraint
grief of the bondmaid
and state of oppression
and toilsome work.

ISA: Ice
bark of rivers
and roof of the wave
and destruction of the doomed.

JERA: Plenty
Boon to men
and good summer
and thriving crops.

EIWAZ: Yew
bent bow
and brittle iron
and giant of the arrow.

SOWELU: Sun
shield of the clouds
and shining ray
and destroyer of ice.

TEIWAZ: Týr
God with one hand

and leavings of the wolf
and Prince of Temples.

BERKANA: Birch
leafy twig
and little tree
and fresh young shrub.

MANNAZ: Man
delight of man
and augmentation of the earth
and adorner of ships.

LAGUZ: Water
eddying stream
and broad geyser
and land of the fish.

The Norwegian Rune Poem (Old Norse)

FEHU: Fé vældr frænda róge;
føðesk ulfr í skóge.

URUZ: Úr er af illu jarne;
opt løypr ræinn á hjarne.

THURISAZ: Þurs vældr kvinna kvillu;
kátr værðr fár af illu.

ANSUZ: Óss er flæstra færða
for; en skalpr er sværða.

RAIDO: Ræið kveða rossom væsta;
Reginn sló sværðet bæzta.

KENAZ: Kaun er barna bolvan;
bo, l gørver nán fo, lvan.

HAGALAZ: Hagall er kaldastr korna;
Kristr skóp hæimenn forna.

NAUTHIZ: Nauðr gerer næppa koste;
nøktan kælr í froste.

ISA: Ís kollum brú bræiða;

	blindan þarf at læiða.
JERA:	Ár er gumna góðe;
	get ek at orr var Fróðe.
EIWAZ:	Ýr er vetrgrønstr viða;
	vænt er, er brennr, at sviða.
SOWELU:	Sól er landa ljóme;
	lúti ek helgum dóme.
TEIWAZ:	Týr er æinendr ása;
	opt værðr smiðr blása.
BERKANA:	Bjarkan er laufgrønstr líma;
	Loki bar flærða tíma.
MANNAZ:	Maðr er moldar auki;
	mikil er græip á hauki.
LAGUZ:	Logr er, fællr ór fjalle
	foss; en gull ero nosser.

The Norwegian Rune Poem (Translation)

FEHU:	Wealth is a source of discord among kinsmen;
	the wolf lives in the forest.
URUZ:	Dross comes from bad iron;
	the reindeer often races over the frozen snow.
THURISAZ:	Giant causes anguish to women;
	misfortune makes few men cheerful.
ANSUZ:	Rivermouth begins most journeys;
	but the scabbard is for the sword.
RAIDO:	Riding is said to be the worst thing for horses;
	Reginn forged the finest sword.
KENAZ:	Ulcer is death to children;
	death makes a corpse pale.
HAGALAZ:	Hail is the coldest of grain;
	Christ created the world of old.
NAUTHIZ:	Constraint gives scant choice;
	a naked man is chilled by the frost.

ISA: Ice we call the broad bridge;
            the blind man must be led.

JERA: Plenty is a boon to men;
            I say that Frothi was generous.

EIWAZ: Yew is the greenest of trees in winter;
            it is wont to crackle when it burns.

SOWELU: Sun is the light of the world;
            I bow to the divine decree.

TEIWAZ: Tyr is a one-handed God;
            often has the smith to blow.

BERKANA: Birch has the greenest leaves of any shrub;
            Loki was fortunate in his deceit.

MANNAZ: Man is an augmentation of the dust;
            great is the claw of the hawk.

LAGUZ: A waterfall is a river which falls from a mountain-
            side; but ornaments are of gold.

Further Runic Alphabets

The runic alphabets evolved over time, as the languages of the users changed, in the same way our own English writing has changed. If you don't know what I mean, try looking for an online image of a hand-written document dating back only a century or so, such as a census entry: it can be almost unreadable to modern eyes. Some letters have changed their shapes considerably, for example the long 'S' of texts from the 18th century and earlier, which looks like a lower-case F, had disappeared from print, if not handwriting, by around 1800.

The early Norsemen spoke ancient, or proto-, Norse and their alphabet was customised for that language and its pronunciation, but as the runes travelled out of Scandinavia and across Europe, they underwent more changes as they encountered other languages. And the Norse language itself evolved, becoming Old Norse.

There were many runic alphabets; however, the three best known are the Elder Futhark, the alphabet we have journeyed with through these pages; the Anglo-Saxon or Old English Futhorc; and the Younger Futhark. The timeline of these alphabets goes like this: Elder Futhark 150CE – 800CE; Anglo-Saxon Futhorc 400CE – 1100CE; and Younger Futhark 800CE – 1100CE; these dates are approximate. The Younger Futhark also had two distinct forms, a taller and a shorter way of writing the staves, and this alphabet went on into the Middle Ages as mediaeval runes and Dalecarlian runes, in which latter form they continued in use until the 19th century.

Futhorc either developed in the area of Northern Germany and the Netherlands called Frisia and then spread to England, or developed in England from Norse runes taken there by invaders and travellers. By this time, the alphabet had grown to 29 letters, and later grew to 33, as the more complex vowel sounds of the Old English language demanded.

As you can see, the Elder Futhark letters are all there, though some have changed their shape slightly. And added to these are some compound consonants (ST and QU), and extra vowel and diphthong sounds, some, like the *gar*-rune, very complex in structure compared to the simple outlines of the original runestaves.

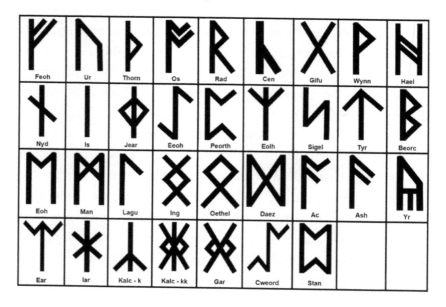

The Younger Futhark alphabet is actually a shorter form of the Elder Futhark, with a third of the letters discarded as the language changed. As you can see, the first six letters that gave the alphabet its name remain largely unchanged — only Kenaz has altered its shape, presumably to bring it more in line with the other upright letters. The letters corresponding to Hagalaz, Ansuz, Mannaz and Raido have changed completely, and Sowelu is often shown turned around and Bjarkan (Berkana) now represents P as well as B, Pertho having been discarded – presumably P was not a common sound in the later language. The outline once assigned to Algiz is now M. Wunjo, Gebo, Jera, Eiwaz, Ingwaz, Ehwaz, Othila and Daggaz are missing altogether, with other letters having taken on their function in some cases. This leaves the runic alphabet much the poorer; in fact, one wonders how they managed to use this depleted version for writing at all, let alone for magic and divination. But as the runes moved on into the mediaeval era, the alphabet expanded again as the German language evolved.

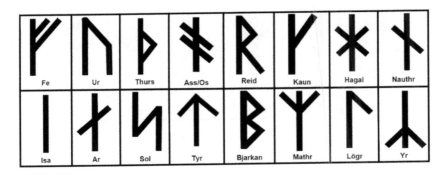

Armanen Runes

As interest in the runes resurged, an Austrian mystic invented his own set, which he published in the early years of the 20th century as an alternative system for use in divination and magic, and as part of his new heathen tradition called Wotanism, a reclaiming tradition that asserted the qabalah was originally a Germanic system. Guido von List claimed he saw the runes in a spiritual revelation while he suffered a period of temporary blindness after an eye operation. The runes are closely based on the two Futhark alphabets and contain 18 runes. Sadly, because List's work was inherently racist, it was seized on by the German and Austrian Nazi parties and became an integral part of their symbology and their occult work.

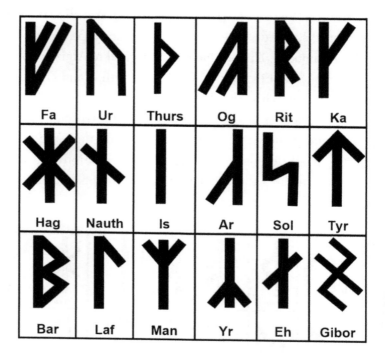

Correspondences and Connections

Like most magical tools and substances, the runes have their own list of *correspondences*, a magical list of connected elements witches use to increase power in their workings. For example, in everyday witchcraft, a magical spell to help you pass an exam in IT might involve the correspondences of Mercury, God of Communication, Science and Intelligence. This would involve using a certain colour of candle, altar cloth and perhaps candle holders as well (in this case orange), using the right incense and the right herbs on the altar, and perhaps even images of animals associated with Mercury.

The runes each have their own set of correspondences. Some of them, especially the colours, look a little odd to our eyes, but if you prefer to stick to classical planetary correspondences, that is fine as long as you are consistent.

The runes also have strong connections to the Tarot, even though they come from different times and cultures, so where there are alignments with the Major or Minor Arcana, I have indicated this. The runes also connect to astrological signs, both the signs of the Zodiac and the planets. Some runes are linked to a time of day – I have seen authors ascribe a definite time, such as '2.30–3.30pm' to a rune, which I feel is a little unrealistic; I don't believe the

Norsemen spent much time checking their watches. However, where I feel a rune has a time of day, I have put it in. Some are also associated with a Sabbat (pagan festival), and I have indicated where this is the case. Feel free to disagree with me; I have assigned the Tarot and astrological correspondences according to my own understanding rather than just copying them from websites, but they may not work for everyone.

Fehu

ELEMENTS:	Earth and Fire.
GODS:	Freyr and Freyja, Njörd, Nerthus, Frigga, Audhumla.
COLOUR:	Gold and light red.
ANIMALS AND PLANTS:	Cattle, cats, elder tree, stinging nettle. This rune was particularly linked to the farming of animals, so any farm animals.
TAROT:	The Empress, the Wheel of Fortune and the Ace of Pentacles.
ASTROLOGY:	Aries, yet I would also think Taurus as well. Jupiter and Pluto.
NUMEROLOGY:	1.
TIME OF DAY:	Late afternoon/sunset.
SABBAT:	The God Freyr, whose rune this is, is deeply associated with the harvest festival of Lughnasadh (Lammas) and also with Yule, when he was born.

Uruz

ELEMENTS:	Earth and Rain
GODS:	Njörd and Thor.
COLOUR:	Green.
ANIMALS AND PLANTS:	The aurochs, all bulls, elm trees, moss.
TAROT:	The Hanged Man.

ASTROLOGY:	Taurus.
NUMEROLOGY:	2.
SABBAT:	Imbolc, as it is associated with initiation.

Thurisaz

ELEMENTS:	Earth and Fire.
GODS:	Thor and Loki.
COLOUR:	Red.
ANIMALS AND PLANTS:	Snakes and scorpions, briar, blackthorn.
TAROT:	The Tower.
ASTROLOGY:	Saturn and Mars.
Numerology:	3.

Ansuz

ELEMENTS:	Air.
GODS:	Odin, reversed Loki.
COLOUR:	dark blue (this is the colour associated with Odin).
ANIMALS AND PLANTS:	Wolf, raven and all flying birds. Ash and elm, fly agaric toadstools – this poisonous fungus is a strange correspondence – until you remember its use by shamans to induce trance states and visions.
TAROT:	The Emperor and the Hermit.
ASTROLOGY:	Mercury.
NUMEROLOGY:	4.

Raido

ELEMENTS:	Air and Fire.
GODS:	Thor and Odin.
COLOUR:	Red.
ANIMALS AND PLANTS:	Goats, horses, oak trees, arnica.

TAROT:	The Chariot and the Emperor.
ASTROLOGY:	Sagittarius/Jupiter and Mercury.
NUMEROLOGY:	5.

Kenaz

ELEMENTS:	Fire.
GODS:	Surtr, Heimdallr, Freyr and Freyja, Völund (Wayland).
COLOUR:	Red and orange.
ANIMALS AND PLANTS:	Dragons, pine, hazel trees, bilberry, Ragged Robin.
TAROT:	The Magician.
ASTROLOGY:	Venus and Mercury.
NUMEROLOGY:	6.
TIME OF DAY:	Midday.
SABBATS:	All the Celtic fire festivals: Imbolc, Beltane, Lughnasadh and Samhain.

Gebo

ELEMENTS:	Water and Air.
GODS:	Odin and Frigga, who is very similar to Hera/Juno in classical belief: representing the values of wifedom, motherhood, hospitality.
COLOUR:	Deep blue.
ANIMALS AND PLANTS:	Ox, ash, elm, wild pansy (eyebright, Euphrasia). Also *any* kinds of flowers, which are usually a part of any celebration and also a gift in themselves, not only from a person to another person, but for the bees and insects that live on the nectar.
TAROT:	Temperance.

ASTROLOGY:	Pisces and Leo.
NUMEROLOGY:	7.
SABBATS:	Lughnasadh and Yule.

Wunjo

ELEMENTS:	Earth and Fire.
GODS:	Freyr.
COLOUR:	Gold or yellow.
ANIMALS AND PLANTS:	Any gregarious animals, flax, chestnuts.
TAROT:	The Sun.
ASTROLOGY:	Leo.
NUMEROLOGY:	8.
SABBAT:	All the celebratory ones, Imbolc, Ostara, Beltane, Lughnasadh, Mabon and Yule

Hagalaz

ELEMENTS:	Earth and Water.
GODS:	Hel and Ymir.
COLOUR:	Ice blue.
ANIMALS AND PLANTS:	Geese, yew, lily of the valley.
TAROT:	The Tower.
ASTROLOGY:	Uranus.
NUMEROLOGY:	9.
TIME OF DAY:	Morning.

Nauthiz

ELEMENTS:	Fire.
GODS:	The Norns, Loki.
COLOUR:	Black.
ANIMALS AND PLANTS:	Squirrels, beech trees, bistort.
TAROT:	The Devil.
ASTROLOGY:	Saturn and Capricorn.
NUMEROLOGY:	10.

Isa

ELEMENTS:	Water.
GODS:	Verdandi and Skadi.
COLOUR:	Black.
ANIMALS AND PLANTS:	Reindeer, snowy owl, alder trees, henbane.
TAROT:	The Devil and the Moon.
ASTROLOGY:	Moon.
NUMEROLOGY:	11.

Jera

ELEMENTS:	Fire and Earth.
GODS:	Freyr.
COLOUR:	Light blue or harvest gold.
ANIMALS AND PLANTS:	Freyr's totem animals the pig and the horse, oak trees, any kind of grain, rosemary. Jera was especially associated with vegetable harvests of grain and other plants, so almost any kind of summer or autumn fruit.
TAROT:	The Empress and the World.
ASTROLOGY:	Point of Fortune.
NUMEROLOGY:	12.
TIME OF DAY:	Afternoon/sunset.
SABBATS:	Lughnasadh, Mabon and Yule, the equinoxes.

Eiwaz

ELEMENTS:	Fire.
GODS:	Odin.
COLOUR:	Black, dark green.
ANIMALS AND PLANTS:	Hedgehogs, herons, yew trees, mandrake.

TAROT: Death and Judgement.
ASTROLOGY: Scorpio.
NUMEROLOGY: 13.
TIME OF DAY: Midnight.
SABBATS: Litha and Samhain.

Pertho

ELEMENTS: Water.
GODS: The Nornir and Frigga.
COLOUR: Black, silver and green.
ANIMALS AND PLANTS: Women, herons, elm trees, belladonna.
TAROT: The Lovers.
ASTROLOGY: Saturn.
NUMEROLOGY: 14.

Algiz

ELEMENTS: Air.
GODS: Heimdallr and the Valkyries.
COLOUR: Silver, green or multi-coloured like the
                       rainbow.
ANIMALS AND PLANTS: Elk, swans, sedges, lime trees, angelica,
                       all protective plants.
TAROT: The Empress.
ASTROLOGY: Pisces.
NUMEROLOGY: 15.

Sowelu

ELEMENTS: Fire.
GODS: Baldr and Sunna.
COLOUR: Yellow and gold.
ANIMALS AND PLANTS: Lions, eagles, juniper, chamomile,
                       mistletoe.
TAROT: The Sun.

ASTROLOGY:	Sun, Leo.
NUMEROLOGY:	16.
TIME:	Daylight.
SABBATS:	Yule, Litha.

Teiwaz

ELEMENTS:	Fire.
GODS:	Tyr.
COLOUR:	Red.
ANIMALS AND PLANTS:	Lions, wolves, crows, eagles, oak trees, wolfsbane.
TAROT:	Justice and strength.
ASTROLOGY:	Mars, Libra, Aries.
NUMEROLOGY:	17.

Berkana

ELEMENTS:	Earth and Water.
GODS:	Nerthus, Frigga and Freyja.
COLOUR:	Green.
ANIMALS AND PLANTS:	ears, swans, birch trees, motherwort. The sacred birch tree was made more special by the association with the fly agaric toadstool, which loves to grow under birch trees and was used by Norse shamans and sorcerers as a hallucinogenic drug, while the fungus was also sacred because of its red and white colouring, which was seen as representing male-female fertility. I am told that birchwood is the traditional choice for a maypole, not to mention the traditional witch's besom.
TAROT:	The High Priestess and the Empress.

ASTROLOGY:	Cancer and Virgo.
NUMEROLOGY:	18.
TIME OF DAY:	Early morning.

Ehwaz

ELEMENTS:	Air.
GODS:	Odin, Sleipnir.
COLOUR:	White or yellow.
ANIMALS AND PLANTS:	Horses, albatrosses, ash trees, ragwort.
TAROT:	The Lovers.
ASTROLOGY:	Gemini, Mercury.
NUMEROLOGY:	19.
SABBATS:	Beltane.

Mannaz

ELEMENTS:	Water and Air.
GODS:	Heimdallr, Huginn and Muninn.
COLOUR:	Red.
ANIMALS AND PLANTS:	Men, hawks, holly trees, mandrake.
TAROT:	The Fool.
ASTROLOGY:	Aquarius.
NUMEROLOGY:	20.

Laguz

ELEMENTS:	Water.
GODS:	Njörd.
COLOUR:	Green.
ANIMALS AND PLANTS:	Seals, ducks and all water creatures, seaweed, leeks, willow trees.
TAROT:	The Star.
ASTROLOGY:	Pisces, Cancer and Scorpio, Neptune, Moon.
NUMEROLOGY:	21.

Ingwaz

ELEMENTS:	Fire.
GODS:	Ingvi-Freyr and Freyja.
COLOUR:	Orange and yellow.
ANIMALS AND PLANTS:	Boar (Freyr's totem animal), cuckoo, apple tree, self-heal.
TAROT:	The Devil and the suit of Cups.
ASTROLOGY:	Black Moon, Venus.
NUMEROLOGY:	22.
SABBATS:	Beltane.

Daggaz

ELEMENTS:	Air.
GODS:	Baldr, Eostre and Verdandi.
COLOUR:	Light blue.
ANIMALS AND PLANTS:	Deer, skylarks, crowing roosters, rowan trees and clary sage.
TAROT:	The World, the Wheel of Fortune.
ASTROLOGY:	Half Moon.
NUMEROLOGY:	23.
TIME OF DAY:	Dawn.
SABBATS:	All of them.

Othila

ELEMENTS:	Fire.
GODS:	Odin.
COLOUR:	Yellow and dark blue.
ANIMALS AND PLANTS:	Ravens, pigeons, salmon, snails, hawthorn, daisy.
TAROT:	The Empress.
ASTROLOGY:	Moon.
NUMEROLOGY:	24.
SABBATS:	Samhain.

Runic Time

Because there are 24 runes, they lend themselves to magical timing or a runic calendar, though it should be emphasized that this is a modern concept and has little or nothing to do with the Norse traditions. Many magical practitioners will be familiar with the concept of *planetary hours*, in which the day or night is divided up into 12 hours, each assigned to a planet, for magical work. This system is based on the Chaldean order of planets, and the start of each day is taken as sunrise and the start of each night as sunset – so some hours are going to be pretty short, as little as 35 minutes in the British daytime in the winter. The time between sunrise and sunset on the chosen day is divided evenly into 12, and the same for the night. Note that the first hour of each day is dedicated to the planet of that day.

This is incredibly tedious to work out, and often the appropriate hour falls at a very difficult time to perform magic (as a more experienced practitioner, I never now use this system, preferring to go by moon phase and other factors). However, the practitioner of runic magic, especially if he or she is happy to forgo sleep, may find the runic hours valuable for magic and the calendar for spiritual timings.

The runic system is simple to work out and remember, as each rune is allocated a period in the day or a half month in the year in the order in which they stand in the Futhark alphabet: Fehu: midnight to 1am, Uruz: 1–2am, Thurisaz: 2–3am... ending with Othila, 11pm – midnight. This is pretty modern and artificial, so practitioners may well prefer to take a starting point that would be more meaningful to the ancients, such as dawn, and calculate the hours from there. Again, this will lead to an imbalance between the daylight hours and the night-time ones as the seasons change, and of course if you are practising in an area far to the north, such as Canada or Scandinavia, you will have this system knocked on its head by the polar night or midnight sun phenomena.

In 1948, Robert Graves published his influential book *The White Goddess*, which has inspired many neopagans and no doubt played a large part in the rise of Druidry and other nature-based streams. In it he perpetrated the notorious Ogham Tree Calendar, in which he arbitrarily assigned 13 of the Ogham tree runes to sections of the year. This concept has come in for some flack since its publication, and I suspect a calendar based on the Norse runes might well deserve the same. However, the fact remains that there are 24 runes and 12 months in the year, and people love patterns.

The Norsemen did not use our modern system based on the solar year, but calculated their months according to the Moon, with the New Moon marking the first day of the month (our word month shares a common etymological root with the German *monat* and comes from the word for the Moon). Their year consisted of 12 lunar months with some additional days added to keep up with the solar year. The solstices and equinoxes were also observed, as they helped to keep the year on track and were also celebrated as modern pagans do with the Eight Sabbats.

I have seen numerous examples of modern runic calendars, all starting on different dates, but it would seem to make sense to me to start the calendar on one of the solstices, probably the winter solstice, when the days start to lengthen again. Each month could then be divided into two halves and assigned to a rune. Fehu is associated with Yule, so it would make sense to start there, with Othila arriving in the half month before Yule at the other end of the year – appropriate as, in our Christian culture, people are to be seen 'going home for Christmas' at this time of year.

Lightning Source UK Ltd.
Milton Keynes UK
UKHW020939080721
386823UK00006B/204

9 781838 132460